New P[...]

from A.C.T.'s Youn[...]

Volume III

THE YOUNG CONSERVATORY AT
AMERICAN CONSERVATORY THEATER

A.C.T.'s Young Conservatory is a professional theater-training program for young people ages eight to eighteen. The emphasis is on the training of an actor and the development of a young person in relationship to their world and to others. The program provides quality theater training for the beginner, exploring theater and acting for the first time, as well as advanced level study for the young person with previous experience. Classes are designed to develop imagination, concentration, working with others, exploration of character, development of technique in acting, and skills of both the body and the voice. Learning to respect people and the creative process are essentials in the program. Some students come to explore and discover, others come to define and refine their talent and technique to take them further in their goal to become a professional actor. The faculty are working theater professionals who are passionate and skilled in their working with young actors. The Young Conservatory seeks to empower young people to strive for excellence in their lives, while embracing an atmosphere of safety that encourages exploration. The training opportunities frequently extend students the opportunity to play the young roles in the professional company, learning firsthand from working artists. The Young Conservatory is particularly devoted to developing in young people an appreciation of theater in the making of a more human world, and in the importance of the place young people have in the future of the American theater. To this end, the Young Conservatory is a center for actor training for young people and development of new theater writing both by young people and by professional playwrights challenged to see the world through the eyes of the young. Critical thinking, feeling, and giving are cornerstones of this twenty-year program.

For Jack Sharrar
and Jerome Moskowitz

NEW PLAYS

From A.C.T.'s
Young Conservatory

Volume III

Edited by Craig Slaight

YOUNG ACTORS SERIES

SK
A Smith and Kraus Book

A Smith and Kraus Book
Published by Smith and Kraus, Inc.
PO Box 127, Lyme, NH 03768

Cover Photo © Bob Adler. From the A.C.T. production of *A Bird of Prey,* by Jim Grimsley.
(From left to right) Nicholas Hongola as a Street Angel, Sarah Ichioka as a Street Angel,
Rio Chavez as a Street Angel, and Travis Engle as Corvette.

First Edition: March 1999
10 9 8 7 6 5 4 3 2 1

Book design by Julia Hill Gignoux, Freedom Hill Design

The Library of Congress Cataloging-In-Publication Data
New Plays from A.C.T.'s Young Conservatory Volume III / Craig Slaight
p. cm. Audiences: Ages 12-22
ISBN 1-57525-122-1

1. American drama--Collections. 2. Plays--Collections.
I. Slaight, Craig. II. American Conservatory Theatre.
III. Title: New Plays from American Conservatory Theatre's Young Conservatory.

PN625.5.N49 1993   812'.5400835
QBI93-20017

CONTENTS

The plays in this volume were originally produced with the generous support from the LEF Foundation and The Fred Gellert Foundation, at American Conservatory Theater.

FOREWORD

Some of the most successful work ever written for the theater was created for specific companies of actors at specific points in their history. But rarely has dramatic literature been specifically created with *young* performers in mind. This is the genius of Craig Slaight's visionary new works program, in which seasoned American playwrights are invited to create theater for the young artists who have trained in A.C.T.'s Young Conservatory. While the plays are not necessarily written with a specific cast in mind, the parameters are clear: Each writer is asked to write something that actively engages the minds and passions of young (eight- to eighteen-year-old) actors. No subject matter is taboo, no safety net is imposed, and no "artificial sweeteners" allowed! The plays are then rigorously rehearsed and presented in a studio theater at A.C.T.

The gift of this kind of commission is two-fold. First, it allows the writers complete creative freedom and enormous support, freed from the pressures of the press and the concerns of the marketing directors. Secondly, it asks them to travel outside of the terrain that they usually inhabit, in order to consider the world of the young. Those of you who have worked with children know that their world is unto itself: It may look like a smaller version of our own, but in fact its rules are different, its fears are complex, its dreams are secret and well-guarded. To create a script in which children themselves perform, as opposed to a children's theater script performed by adults for children, is to shed preconceptions and travel through the mirror to the other side. The plays in this volume accomplish that journey in very different ways, from Jim Grimsley's terrifying look at the alienation of urban youth to Lynne Alvarez's lyrical look at the distance we will travel for love in *Analiese*. But all four of these plays share a richness of scope, a daring imagination, and a fierce belief in listening to the voices of people under twenty. The afternoons in which I have watched these plays being performed at A.C.T. have been among my happiest times as artistic director, because each one has truly taken me to places I had never been, or brought me back to experiences I had almost forgotten. All of us at A.C.T. are thrilled to share them with you.

Carey Perloff
Artistic Director
American Conservatory Theater

A Bird of Prey

by Jim Grimsley

From the A.C.T. production of *A Bird of Prey*, by Jim Grimsley.
(from left) Rahman Jamaal, Sarah Ichioka, Tegan Holly, Rebecca White,
Adam Jacobs, Michael Smith, Travis Engle, Nicholas Hongola,
Chelsea Peretti, Keller Holmes, and Rio Chavez.
Photo by Bob Adler.

ORIGINAL PRODUCTION

A Bird of Prey was commissioned and first produced by the Young Conservatory New Plays Program at American Conservatory Theater (Carey Perloff, Artistic Director), San Francisco, California, in August, 1996. It was directed by Craig Slaight; costumes by Callie Floor; sound by Phil Stockton; technical direction and lighting by James Bock; and the assistant director was Jeffrey Grigg.

THE STREET ANGELS . . . . Rio Chavez
Nicholas Hongola
Sarah Ichioka
THACKER . . . . Michael Smith
TRACEY . . . . Chelsea Peretti
HILDA . . . . Keller Holmes
DONNA . . . . Rebecca White
MONTY . . . . Adam Jacobs
MARIE . . . . Tegan Holly
EVAN . . . . Rahman Jamaal
CORVETTE . . . . Travis Engle

PLAYWRIGHT'S NOTE:

A few years ago, after somebody named Craig Slaight got in touch with me, wondering whether I would be interested in discussing a commission to write a play for his youth conservatory's new works program at A.C.T. in San Francisco, I agreed to have lunch with this fellow the next time I was in town. As it happened, I was in San Francisco in January 1996, and I met Craig Slaight and we had lunch, which turned out to be undercooked chicken at a very nice restaurant.

Craig described a program that seemed unbelievable to me at the time, the opportunity to write a play for a large ensemble of actors ranging in age from eight to eighteen, and to work on the play with Craig and the actors over the course of two to four weeks in preparation for a weekend of workshop performances at the theater. As a playwright I have never been told I could write for as many actors as I wanted. When I asked what kind of play I would be expected to write, Craig's answer was that I should write whatever I wanted, that he would impose no limitations or expectations. As it turned out, that would be the answer to all my questions. This was a project that would be up to me to shape.

A lot of events transpired after I said yes to the project, culminating in my agreeing to write a play for that same year, to have a draft of the play by June, to all of which I agreed wholeheartedly in spite of the fact that I had a lot going on in my own life, at the time. But I got the play done on schedule, more or less, and sent it away, and we got to work on it.

Came July and I fled the Olympic city, Atlanta, the day after opening ceremonies for the Games, which I did not attend. I spent the next two weeks rewriting, talking to Craig, and working with the gifted actors Craig had cast in my play, and then came back three weeks later to see the performance that was the result of our work.

The play that we made is presented here, so I will not say much about it except to note that the actors, an incredibly gifted bunch, performed it with such grace and heart that the hard subject matter of the play became, for me, filled with the hopefulness of the people who were acting in it. I have never had a better experience doing a play and we still, Craig and the actors and I, all stay in touch with one another as we can.

—*Jim Grimsley*

DIRECTOR'S NOTE

I have playwright Horton Foote to thank for my introduction to Jim Grimsley. Sometime ago, Horton called me to say that he had just finished reading a brilliant short novel by a very bright young Southern writer. Horton felt that the story would be particularly interesting to me because the point of view was that of an eight-year-old boy, and that it was a startling, unsentimental, and piercing tale of a small child living in complete terror— too young to do anything to stop the rage of a father out of control, raining psychological and physical abuse upon the children and their gracious, loving mother. This book was *Winter Birds,* Jim Grimsley's first novel. I defer to Horton when he suggests anything to read and so I bought *Winter Birds* that very day and finished it that evening. Horton was right, this fellow, Grimsley, was indeed a gifted new voice. I had never before read a story told by one so young with such truth and clarity. Not only had Grimsley spread out the world before us, seen from the vantage point of eight-year-old eyes, he had somehow found this boy's soul and was able to make it live compellingly for all time. I had been led to a fiction writer who genuinely understood young lives, remembering his own experience with profound and unique results (the novel had autobiographical roots), with the translucence of a camera lens. He had reclaimed his vision for all of us. We could crawl into Danny's eight-year-old soul and experience the sharp smell of fear and the helplessness of youth. When I turned to the back of the book, I found in Mr. Grimsley's brief and self-effacing bio that he was a playwright as well as a novelist. In that instant a door was opened to me, a door that would lead to *A Bird of Prey.*

While I waited for Mr. Grimsley's second novel to appear, I made some inquiries and approached his agent with a simple request: Could I read some of Jim Grimsley's plays? A short stack of scripts followed and I read, with surprise, three plays that were quite wonderful, but none that contained the youthful voice I had heard in *Winter Birds.* Perhaps, I thought, the autobiographical nature of the novel was a one-time urge to speak through the child, as he so vividly had done with young Danny.

Then *Dream Boy,* Grimsley's second novel, landed in my hands. Here was a novel as arresting as *Winter Birds.* And once more, here was a young character (this time in his teens), who lived in a dangerous world, manipulated by a terrifying, alcoholic father, and a helpless, benevolent mother. Added to the danger was the complex issue of a gay teen's coming of age and grappling with his awakening sexuality. This astringent and compelling story was unlike any other novel, play, essay, or poem I had ever read dealing with such issues. Like *Winter Birds*, this novel was just over two hundred pages, yet contained a richness of ideas and language, and a complexity of character and drama. This was a writer for me. This was a voice for the New Plays Program.

When I finally met Jim Grimsley, he was battling illness and a fatiguing schedule. We quickly fell into a discussion about our shared passion for play development. He was as intrigued with our program as I was impressed with his work. We agreed to work on a project together. I asked him about the difference in the youthful voices of his two novels and the adult world of his plays. Jim said that in his novels he had always felt free to write exactly what he wanted—but with plays, he felt he needed to appeal to the adult world that would produce those plays. I asked Jim to write a play that followed the path taken in his novels and requested only that the play be seen through youthful eyes. Paula Vogel was writing a new play for our upcoming summer and so Jim and I agreed that we would work the following year on our project. I soon learned, however, that as Vogel continued to work on her new play, it was evolving into a more exclusively adult story. In time, Paula and I agreed that she had found the right direction with the play, and that another project would ultimately bring us together. (That play became *How I Learned to Drive,* which has had a wondrous life and won Ms. Vogel the Pulitzer Prize.) I put down the phone from my conversation with Paula Vogel and immediately picked it up again and dialed Jim Grimsley. Jim said he needed a few days to consider an earlier start date. He had, of course, thought he would have a year to contemplate his project. The next day he called and said, "Let's do it." He had a story in mind, one that involved a group of teens, living on the edge in a metropolitan city, grappling with good and evil on their own terms. He also wanted to explore the meaning of genuine faith. And so our journey took focus.

We began with a draft that included most of the scenes in order, but still unfinished. It was after we began rehearsals that Jim introduced the Street Angels—this trio of poetic souls who strive to have a hand in rescuing the crumbling world of lonely, desperate youth. It was as if these Street Angels could not rest until they had affected some essential change. As Jim and I worked the Street Angels into the play, we devised a look that would set a visual presence. These were not beatific cherubs who appear to the living with comfort or prophecy. Our Street Angeles were troubled spirits, struck down in their youth, destined to exist restlessly longing to help the living. Even their speech was not of this world, but written in free verse. Additionally, Jim felt that the Street Angels should carry boom boxes and that all of the sound effects could be played by them live. I conceived a costume that included military vests, the pockets altered to carry the cassette tapes. Instead of carrying the boom box, I had our Angels wear them with colorful straps—creating a look that resembled soldiers carrying weapons. As the music was required, the Angels would *load* their boom boxes and actually use the music as an attempt to permeate the invisible wall between them and the living. This gave a haunting presence to the Angels and helped them serve as the catalyst that drives the characters through the events of the story. With the addition of this other-world element to the play, the size of the work and the compelling stakes it created made us all feel we were involved with something that would have a far-reaching effect.

This was not the easiest play I have ever directed—not because the play is so inherently complicated in theatrical terms—but rather because the lives of the characters are so fragile, so desperate, so sad. Rehearsals were quiet, focused, intense. As we wrestled with the world seen through Grimsley's eyes, the sadness of that world descended upon us, challenging everyone to reconsider our sometimes flippant journeys through our own lives. Our rehearsal breaks were childish and resembled a buzzing playground—welcome joyous pause between truthful theater making. Finally, the performances yielded the promise of the original notion: Grimsley the visionary voice of young people offered in the world of a theater that knows no age. Performance after performance, rows of young people sat in front of rows of older people. I have never before seen a response to match what we saw with our truly multigenerational audiences. Adults stopped me to say "every teenager should see this play." I agreed, adding, "with their parents."

A Bird of Prey is an important play by an important writer. We were all honored to have taken the maiden voyage. Now you have the opportunity to travel with the Angels.

—*Craig Slaight*

ACTOR'S NOTE

Week one of rehearsals hadn't even begun yet. I was given a copy of the script and was told to take a look at it. So, I read it over and started contemplating two of the characters—Monty and Thacker. What makes them who they are? Why do they exist in the play? What purpose do they have? What do they want? All kinds of questions were looming in my head and I was trying to have them answered so that when Craig (the director) had me read for the part, I'd be ready.

The next day I saw him in his office. "So, Craig, any new news about the play?" "Yeah." He sounded excited. "I was thinking of having you play Corvette. What do you think?" I mulled it over. Corvette. Who the hell is Corvette I thought? Isn't that a car? "Sure! I'd love to." "Great," he said. And with that, rehearsals were underway.

The incomplete fifty-page script that was in my possession, that over time became the sixty-five pages we were all too familiar with, sat in front of me. Scribbled on the first page was, "For Travis...Good luck with Corvette; with best wishes...Jim Grimsley (the playwright)."

My work and research began. As the five weeks went by at their rapid pace, Corvette developed his form. His feminine strut, spiky chopped hair and naughty, facetious attitude made him his own. I got to know him as a nomadic young man in his own private, twisted world, searching for answers that were nonexistent. And because of his pain, he grew very bitter.

Early on, Craig handed out some clippings of various newspaper and magazine articles that he thought might be helpful in our research. One of which was from a recent *The New Yorker,* called *Elusive Evil.* There were a few quotations that popped out at me that soon became simply the thought of my character; his mantra. "...It is the nature of evil to be *secret*...hurtful behavior becomes self-assertion, even self-salvation...The essence of evil, perhaps, is *not* to know itself." Even in the play, within his post-death speech, his mantra was exposed, "...It's a mean, nasty, evil world..." I then understood that Jim truly did mean, "...good luck with Corvette." Craig as the director was most enjoyable to work with, and gave me, personally, an enormous amount of space to discover who my character would become. But this distance wasn't solely between me and Craig. In fact, I felt it with everyone. What I discovered was that this was how Corvette lived. He was very private and secluded and felt comfortable remaining in his own world. The more Corvette unraveled, the more alone I became. But this wasn't a bad thing because once this young man interacted with the other characters, all seemed to fall into place.

The performances were fresh and exciting, each with new journeys and many more discoveries. And with the three Angels, played by Nick, Sarah, and Rio, watching over us throughout the play, we all took flight. In a matter of just a few days, we landed beautifully.

—*Travis Engle* (Corvette)

ACTOR'S NOTE

Jim Grimsley's *A Bird of Prey* was the second play in A.C.T.'s New Plays Program that I was invited to join. I walked into the Hastings Studio Theater with the light step of expectation. This summer, there were familiar faces at the first rehearsal. We hugged and joked with one another. We caught each other up on our recent artistic and social involvements, peering curiously at the other actors gathered around the table. I was intrigued by the playwright. He seemed relaxed and comfortable in a room full of young adults. He sat beside our director Craig Slaight, conferring with him, laughing, checking us out. His face was angelic, his voice and smile: soft and sweet. But there was a depth in his eyes that revealed him to be more complicated than the average Rafael cherub. He would be more appropriately compared to one of the angels of his creation in *A Bird of Prey*—an angel capable of beautifully wicked laughter. But we learned that later. That first day, before everybody even knew one another, the room was charged. I had a feeling that this summer the workshop and the production would be particularly strong.

The script certainly did not alter this initial impression. As we read Mr. Grimsley's work aloud, we read a transcription of our own world. His play did not attempt to simplify or idealize the young adult experience. His characters and their lives were as textured as our own. This was no episode of *Saved by the Bell*. Thacker was up against the wall in a way that popular teen characters such as Slater are not allowed to be. *A Bird of Prey* was an introspective *West Side Story*, hold the song and dance. I was cast as Tracey. I read my first lines that afternoon. Tracy was guarded, mean, loud, scared. She loved her friends. She loved to hurt her enemies. She was viciously funny. She competed savagely for attention on life's expansive stage. Like the other characters, she was surrounded by people but hauntingly alone. Grimsley's youth were frenetically scattered across the page. He resisted order, formulas. For us, no Daddy Warbucks came to save the day. We had no one to talk to. We were nervous amongst ourselves. Our parents were distant, alien. Corvette sold his body. Thacker sold his drugs. Monty read and reread his bible. As Tracey, all I had was my sharp tongue. In the laughter of my peers I found solace, temporary family. I was going to classes with butterflies in my stomach, Corvette's hell being the feared graduation. Unlike most commercial teen characters, my future was not even guaranteed to come.

Tracey is a complex character who I will never forget. She says at one point: "Maybe the whole world is a big waste of time, and I'm the only one in it who is mean enough to say so." As an actor, I had to decide how to interpret this line. Was her life truly utter boredom and pointless? Or did she describe it that way because she was emotionally guarded, or disillusioned? Her nonrevelation speech further nurses this question. Here, Tracey addresses the expectant audience, alone onstage: "I'm supposed to have this big revelation, right?…Crap…The truth is, I feel exactly like I said I feel." *Does* she feel exactly as she says she feels? Her tragic monologue in the final scene provides insight. It is Tracey who reveals Thacker's involvement in Corvette's death to the audience. She describes feeling sick to her stomach. She says of Thacker, "I knew he was like that, sick inside." She says: "I felt so sorry." These lines were hugely responsible for my interpretation of Tracey. They show that maybe her world *is* a big waste of time, and maybe she sees herself and Thacker and her peers as infected, sick. But she is sorry. Little Tracey with the big mouth is sorry. Even in a pointless, disappointing world, she doesn't want Corvette to die. His death makes her "feel." Her sickness and her sorrow are the only things she professes to feel, ever. I chose to use this short speech to reveal a break in Tracy's surface. It was an immense opportunity. I was finally able to release some of the great tension this proud character carries inside her small frame. It didn't have to be the commercial revelation she scorned in her earlier monologue. At that point, a break in her cruel demeanor would have been a concession to the optimists in the audience. The placement of this opening in her character, and the way it is written, make her vulnerability difficult to swallow. And so Mr. Grimsley's audience watches in silence. The cynic is right, and wishes that she were wrong. The final chorus provides no consolation:

Sometimes I feel like crying, I don't know
why I would do it or where I would sit
and if somebody found me I don't know what
I would say, something stupid I guess.

The easiest words I could think of, I'm lonely
I wish I had someone to talk to
some days I get so crazy inside.

—*Chelsea Peretti* (Tracey)

CHARACTERS

MONTY: seventeen or eighteen. Conservative dresser, clothes ridiculed by peers. Shirts and ties; tie clips; trousers rather than jeans, looking as though they originally belonged to someone larger. Carries a Bible among his schoolbooks. Called Starch by people at school.

THACKER: seventeen or eighteen, smooth and cool, charming, wearing the right kind of clothes, but an outsider despite this. Carries a beeper.

CORVETTE: sixteen or seventeen, a pretty boy, possessed by his own appetites. Later, dead.

HILDA: fifteen to seventeen, a girl on the fringe of popularity, slightly in love with Tracey, not yet fully conscious of it at the beginning of the play

TRACEY: fifteen to seventeen, a girl with a harsh view of people and the ability to express it, but very loyal to her friends

DONNA: fifteen to seventeen, mostly seen with Hilda and Tracey but doesn't quite fit with them, morbid, superstitious, drawn to Monty

EVAN: sixteen, Monty's brother, a handsome kid, very angry about his family

MARIE: fifteen, Monty's sister, confused about herself, about the move her family made, about the new kids around her; picked on by Evan

THE STREET ANGELS: who are invisible, who appear and disappear, who carry boom boxes, who are a chorus and orchestra

SETTING/STAGE

Flexible stage that can represent various public areas: school athletic field, school common area, steps outside apartment building, park, churchyard, etc. The stage should allow for many different playing levels and areas and is largely bare and unadorned. The play takes place in an unnamed city in the 1990s.

A Bird of Prey

Angel voices are heard in darkness.

ANGEL VOICE: Does anybody hear the angels when they speak, does anybody
ANGEL VOICE: see us, does anybody see the angels, will anybody
ANGEL VOICE: understand us, is it any use to try to try again, can anything
ANGEL VOICE: make a difference?
   (Lights have risen slowly revealing the Street Angels, standing with their boom boxes on different areas of the stage.)
ANGELS IN UNISON: Does anybody hear the angels when we are talking, does anybody see us, we are haunting you, does anybody see the angels will anybody understand us? We are doing the best we can do. Is it any use to try again, to tell this story again can anything make a difference?
   (Street Angels move toward the entrances from which the other characters will appear. The Angels have turned on their boom boxes and sounds are heard, school bells, young voices speaking Spanish, English, other languages. Music mixed in with the voices. Rhythms and instruments in confusion. Car horns, gunshots, teachers talking about geography and auto mechanics. Enter Thacker. His Angel bows his head. Thacker sees nothing, takes his place and slouches. He has neither books nor lunch, he stares straight ahead. Enter Hilda and Tracey. Their Angel stares at them, follows them, turns up the boom box loud and holds it toward Tracey as if the Angel would like her to hear. Hilda and Tracey sit on an upper level of the platform. Enter Donna. Her Angel takes her hand and leads her toward Tracey and Hilda. She almost recognizes the Angel, then forgets when she sits down with them. They are eating lunch. Enter Monty with his schoolbooks, a small Bible, and his lunch. The Angels bow their heads toward him, lift their boom boxes, sound swells. The Angels move toward their exits without turning away from Monty. At the same moment they turn off the sound.)
ANGELS: Is it any use to try again, to tell this story again. Can a story make a difference?
   (Angels vanish in different directions at the same moment. The girls, watching Monty, have been whispering, making fun of him, and giggle so he will know it.)

TRACEY: Hey, Starch. Looking for a place to eat?

MONTY: Hi.

TRACEY: Good-looking tie, Starch.

(Monty would like to approach them and makes motion in that direction but is hesitant.)

MONTY: You don't like the way I dress, do you?

HILDA: I think it's great. Those pants are great. Where did you get them?

TRACEY: It's the shoes I like. Did you have those in Arkansas?

MONTY: I'm not from Arkansas.

TRACEY: Do they all carry a Bible around in Arkansas?

(Monty does not answer.)

TRACEY: Answer me. Do all the people carry a Bible where you come from?

MONTY: No.

TRACEY: So why do you?

DONNA: She's just giving you a hard time. Starch.

(Monty watches Donna when she calls him this name. She cannot look at him but studies her lunch.)

TRACEY: No, I'm, like, interested. I really want to know.

HILDA: She's religious too.

TRACEY: Right. I'm religious. *(Pause.)* So, do you like get inner strength from it, or something?

HILDA: Or fashion instructions?

(Girls giggle, including Donna.)

MONTY: It doesn't matter.

TRACEY: What?

MONTY: Why I carry it. It doesn't matter. *(He is starting to move away from them toward Thacker.)* I don't carry it to talk about.

TRACEY: Oh. *(Pause.)* I thought maybe it was something spiritual. You know, like God told you to do it or something.

MONTY: *(Stopped in his movement by this.)* It is something spiritual.

TRACEY: Then what is it?

MONTY: You're making fun of me again.

HILDA: No, she's not.

TRACEY: No, I'm not. I really want to know.

MONTY: I like to read it.

TRACEY: Really? Why?

MONTY: It makes me feel calm. Like I can do things.

(Girls giggle.)

HILDA: Do things? Like what?

MONTY: *(Shrugging.)* Just things. Things that are hard.

TRACEY: Do you pray and stuff?

MONTY: I pray. Sure.

TRACEY: Why don't you pray right now?

(Girls laugh.)

TRACEY: I mean it. Lead us in prayer, you know, like this is a church or something.

(Monty walks away without answering. He heads toward Thacker.)

HILDA: We could sing some hymns too. I never did that. Where are you going?

TRACEY: Hey Starch, you don't want to go over there. Stay away from Thacker, he's worse than we are.

THACKER: Yeah, that's right, Thacker is a son of Satan. Don't bring any Bible around him, he'll set it on fire.

(Monty sits a few feet from Thacker and opens his lunch. A white bread sandwich. Potato chips wrapped in a paper towel. The Girls note the white bread and point it out to each other. Donna is becoming uncomfortable with the ridicule but continues to sit with Tracey and Hilda.)

THACKER: *(Speaking in a tone that includes only Monty, not the girls.)* So you're not afraid of me, huh? *(No answer; pause.)* Hey Starch, your lunch looks worse than mine did.

MONTY: My lunch is fine.

THACKER: I haven't seen anybody eat white bread in, god, a hundred thousand years.

MONTY: My mama doesn't buy that brown stuff, she doesn't trust it. That wheat stuff.

THACKER: Your mama?

(Monty nods.)

THACKER: That's what you call her?

MONTY: What do you call your mama?

THACKER: My mother. Mom.

(Monty shrugs.)

THACKER: Hey, I'm not making fun of you. It's just interesting, that's all. The way people from different places use different words for the same thing.

MONTY: In Louisiana we say my mama.

THACKER: You from Louisiana? Everybody around says you came from Arkansas.

MONTY: *(Shaking his head.)* I never even been to Arkansas. I'm from Broussard, south of Lafayette.

(Pause; Thacker has never heard of either place.)

MONTY: On highway 90 west of New Orleans. But I never been to New Orleans.

THACKER: I know where that is. It's at the end of this shitkicking river, right? And there were all kinds of slaves and pirates there.

MONTY: The Mississippi River.

THACKER: Right.

(Silence. Monty has finished his lunch, wipes his mouth with the paper towel, folds the bag neatly and sticks it between books for re-use.)

THACKER: You want a cigarette?

MONTY: No.

THACKER: You don't smoke, do you?

MONTY: My dad does.

THACKER: I do everything bad. Everything. *(Pause.)* You really have a Bible with you?

(Monty holds it up, a little shy.)

THACKER: Wow. I thought they were joking. *(Pause.)* You religious or something?

MONTY: I just have it. That's all.

THACKER: No, really. I want to know. *(Pause, laughs uncomfortably.)* I could use a little God sometimes. You know? Why do you carry it around?

MONTY: I like to read it. *(Pause.)* It makes me feel calmer. Like the part where Jesus spoke to the woman at the well and when he talked to the children. And at the end where he says he will wipe away every tear. I only like the Jesus parts, not all those letters to the Ephesians and stuff like that.

THACKER: Your family go to church or something?

MONTY: No. Just me. Sometimes I take my brother and sister. But mostly it's me. And I can't go all the time. *(Pause.)* How come you eat lunch by yourself? Kids around here don't like you, do they?

THACKER: *(Laughing, with a tone of warning.)* No, they don't.

MONTY: Why not?

THACKER: I told you. I do everything bad.

MONTY: Like what? Like smoking cigarettes?

THACKER: *(Standing.)* Like stuff you don't want to know about. *(Pause.)* So, you think it might help me to read that Bible book sometime?

MONTY: I don't know.

THACKER: Probably not, huh?

(Thacker stands, preparing to exit. Tracey and Donna are also finished with lunch and preparing to leave.)

TRACEY: *(Seeing Thacker.)* Hey, Thack. You got a new boyfriend over there?

THACKER: Cut the crap, Tracey.

TRACEY: I just wondered. I know you need all the friends you can get.

THACKER: I don't need friends like you.

TRACEY: You're right about that. You need friends like Starch. Maybe he can help you see Jesus, right?

(Exit Tracey and Donna.)

THACKER: *(Exiting in another direction.)* Later, Starch.

MONTY: See you.

(Monty continues to sit. After a moment he opens the Bible and reads. Lights around him dim as the Street Angels enter. The Angels sit on one platform in dim light and Hilda moves to their center. The boom boxes are playing quietly. Lights rise on Hilda, who speaks directly to the audience.)

HILDA: I don't hate him or anything. I mean, he's geeky. But there's something cute about him. I can't tell him that, because of Tracey, but I don't hate him, I don't even enjoy making fun of him. Well, not all that much. I enjoy listening to Tracey when she makes fun of him because she's so good at it. I guess that's why I sit there. I guess that's why I join in. He's not the first person Tracey's gone after like that. She always gets after Thacker, but I think it's because she used to like him. She wanted to go out with him, and he wouldn't, or something. She never said anything but I can tell. But with Monty, it's like he's special for her. Ever since he got here. She goes out of her way to let him know how weird he is. I mean, nobody dresses like him, not around here. He only has two ties and he wears them over and over. He must polish his shoes every night. Tracey says he must. She asked him if he uses spit on them, to get that shine. She says there's not a natural fiber on him. *(Laughs a little.)* It's not what she says, it's the way she says it. *(Pause.)* But most of the time he acts as if she isn't saying anything at all. And all you have to do is take one look at him and you know, he doesn't care whether he fits in or not. He's like a sleepwalker, I think. It's like he's not really there. *(Pause.)* I shouldn't encourage Tracey to keep after him, laughing at everything she says the way I do. I wouldn't like it if somebody treated me like that. But I just sit there. *(Pause.)* Mom hates Tracey, she says Tracey's a bad influence. She's not really my mom, she's my step-mom. Whenever I bring Tracey over, she gets this attitude, she treats Tracey really cold. I don't know what I think about the whole thing. Tracey never makes fun of me. She's nice to me. She sticks up for me at school, with the other kids. I don't think I'm wrong to like her so much. But I don't know.

(Lights dim on Hilda. She exits. The Angels stand, two Angels exit, one remains. Angel moves toward Monty as he reads.)

ANGEL: If I could tell you everything I know

    speak in a quiet voice, words like a summer rain

    something to touch you, murmuring like those pages

    explaining how I almost sat here once, in this same place

    how I had a hunger to read a book, but it didn't last

    If I could tell you all I've learned since then

    waiting for heaven, wanting to change the world

    but words don't travel far enough sometimes

    even an angel's voice never travels far enough

    (Enter Evan and Marie. Monty stands. Angel withdraws. Monty hugs Marie but Evan backs away.)

EVAN: Don't be hugging me.

MARIE: I thought Mama was coming.

MONTY: Not today.

    (Marie, Evan, and Monty head offstage as Thacker and Corvette enter.)

THACKER: *(To Monty, in passing.)* End of the day, huh, man? Who are these guys? You got kids?

MONTY: This is my brother and sister, I walk them home.

THACKER: Right. You ought to come out to the park, later.

MONTY: The park?

THACKER: Yeah. Me and some of the guys I know will be out there. Come on by, I'll show you where to find some fun.

MONTY: Not tonight, I have stuff to do tonight.

THACKER: Stuff?

MONTY: Yeah.

THACKER: You going to church or something?

MONTY: No. But I have to stay home.

    (Monty, Evan, and Marie move to the exit.)

THACKER: *(Shrugs.)* Yeah. Oh well. See you later, man. Keep it clean tonight.

MONTY: You, too.

THACKER: Oh, no way. Never. *(Pause; to Corvette, when Monty is offstage.)* Funny little guy. I kind of like him.

CORVETTE: Where does he get those clothes? They look secondhand to me.

THACKER: Maybe. *(Shrugs.)* What's it matter?

CORVETTE: Man, I couldn't dress like that unless I was dead.

THACKER: You don't get to dress yourself when you're dead. You're just dead.

CORVETTE: Right. *(Pause.)* You're not thinking about taking him to the Thunderman, are you?

(Thacker is immediately wary when Corvette says this name. Checks to make sure they are alone. Pulls Corvette to the side.)

THACKER: You stupid little pussy, I told you not to talk about that.

CORVETTE: Hey, there was nobody around.

THACKER: I don't care who's around, when I say you don't talk about it, you don't talk.

CORVETTE: Calm down, Thacker.

THACKER: This is not some game, Corvette. You run your mouth about that stuff and you won't have a mouth to run for long.

CORVETTE: Sorry. *(Pause.)* When are we going back?

THACKER: *(With a soft laugh, like a sneer.)* You like that shit, don't you?

CORVETTE: *(Shy.)* I had a good time. Anything wrong with that?

THACKER: Heavy shit.

CORVETTE: What's wrong with me liking the guy?

THACKER: Could be dangerous. You don't want to fall in love or anything.

CORVETTE: I'm not in love. *(Pause.)* So when can we go over there again?

(Thacker studies Corvette for a long time but says nothing. Something menacing in the way he watches.)

CORVETTE: Jesus, man, you give me the creeps. Answer me.

THACKER: When he says he wants you to come back. That's when.

CORVETTE: How long will that be?

THACKER: Could be a while. Could be tonight. You never know.

(Silence. The Angels approach, surrounding Thacker and Corvette.)

THACKER: You're way too eager for this stuff, man.

CORVETTE: You think so?

THACKER: I think so. *(Pause.)* Do you ever wonder about yourself? About what you're doing?

CORVETTE: I wonder about myself all the time.

THACKER: Yeah?

CORVETTE: But what good does it do? You know?

THACKER: I guess.

CORVETTE: You sound like you're depressed or something.

THACKER: Oh no, not me. *(Pause.)* But I wonder what it would be like, if my mom really knew about all this mess I do. Sometimes. If she really knew what I was doing, I wonder if she would even say anything.

CORVETTE: You scared she's going to find out?

THACKER: Not really.

CORVETTE: Your mom is pretty cool. She probably wouldn't care.

THACKER: Maybe she would.

CORVETTE: What do you want her to know about you, anyway?

THACKER: Everything. I wish she knew everything. I wish she wanted to know everything I do. I wish I didn't have any secrets.

CORVETTE: That sounds pretty stupid.

THACKER: You think so?

CORVETTE: You got to have secrets from your parents. For their sake. They don't want to know what's real.

THACKER: *(Checking his beeper.)* Maybe it is. Stupid, I mean.

CORVETTE: *(Referring to the beeper.)* Is that him?

THACKER: It's none of your business who it is. Come on, I got to find a phone.

CORVETTE: Hey, I thought you didn't want to have any secrets.

(Thacker and Corvette exit. The Angels sit, close together, waiting, as Marie enters to one of the upper levels and faces the audience.)

MARIE: I'm going home, I'm walking behind Monty and Evan, and I'm being quiet so Evan won't punch me in the shoulder, I'm going home like I'm supposed to, but I don't want to go. All day in school it's been peaceful, with nobody bothering me, except Marie in my math class who hates that we have the same name. Except for her they leave me alone, and I like that. All day I sit there with my books and do what I'm supposed to do. Everything is calm all day. But school doesn't last long enough, I have to go home at the end of every day, and when the bell rings I get all hollow inside, and I pack up my books and go outside to wait for Monty and Evan. We walk home the long way, we go pretty slow, and we never talk, unless we're arguing about something. We're all thinking the same thing, we're all wondering what it will be like when we get home, and I hate that feeling, I hate not knowing. I wish it would be peaceful, I think about it the whole way home, and sometimes it is. Sometimes Mama comes to walk us home instead of Monty, and I can tell by the way she looks whether it's okay at home or not. If she's smiling and she's brushed her hair and if she looks me in the eye, then everything's all right. But if she's standing there with her arms all wrapped around herself and her hair pulled back and she's looking at the ground, I know it's not okay, I know they're fighting again. I don't want to go home then, more than anything. But I don't have any choice. I wish school lasted longer. Sometimes I wish it lasted so long I would have to spend the night. I told that to my friend Candy, we have most of our classes together, and she likes me; I told her I wish I could stay in school all the time, but she didn't understand. She says I need a boyfriend, that's all I need, but I think about my dad and I don't know if I want one or not.

(Marie lingers on stage as lights on her go down. Sounds rise from the boom boxes as she finishes. Marie exits, and Angel one shadows her partway. Angel one stops and faces the audience.)

ANGEL ONE: Do you remember us? Do any of you
remember any of us, from before
do you recognize me, do you remember
my face in the newspaper, the story of my death
you must have read about it
do you remember

(Angel two rises, moves into place.)

ANGEL TWO: How I vanished so young, do you remember
the way I looked when they found me
do you remember my face, I had a story
you must have heard it, you must have read about it, I was never
supposed to disappear so early, in broad daylight
can you imagine

(Angel three rises, moves into place.)

ANGEL THREE: How I feel now? Every day haunting the same place
watching the same things happen
wishing for some merciful father to appear
wishing for some heavenly mother's caress
but it's only us, we're the only angels.
Do you remember us? Do you ever
tell the story of the way we died, you must have heard
do you ever think about it?

(Corvette enters and stands in their formation. He is beginning to sense their presence, to be able to see them. The Angels speak while watching him.)

ALL ANGELS: Sometimes I feel like I'm waiting for something to happen
counting the minutes, wondering, sometimes, what it will be
when it comes I don't want it
some days I'm sure I'm not going to make it
I'm moving too fast
some days
and if an angel reached out to me
said, stop, don't do it, don't go in there

if I heard the voice of an angel clear as your voice
if I heard it say, stop
I would keep moving, I know it,
nothing would make any difference

CORVETTE: Sometimes I feel like I'm waiting for something to happen
counting the minutes, wondering, sometimes, what it will be
even if I heard the voice of an angel, clear as your voice
even if an angel said, stop, don't do it
even if an angel said, stop, don't do it
(Blackout, sudden and complete darkness. Sound stop, sudden and complete silence. Tracey and Donna are heard. They enter as lights rise.)

TRACEY: He probably ran away. I mean, you said he hated his parents.

DONNA: But he didn't take any of his clothes.

TRACEY: This is so weird. I mean, I didn't even like the guy.

DONNA: I always thought he was cute.

TRACEY: Sure. But he was gay, wasn't he? And sort of, dumb. I always thought he was dumb.

DONNA: You always think everybody is dumb.

TRACEY: I'm not wrong, most of the time.

DONNA: This is so eerie. I was walking down the hall this afternoon and it was empty and I felt like somebody was watching me. I knew it was my imagination but I still felt like that.

TRACEY: You think somebody kidnapped him or killed him or something?

DONNA: I sure don't think he ran away. Not without any clothes or any of his things. His mom said he went out of the house to see a movie with a friend and he never came back. She woke up early in the morning and he wasn't in the house and his bed wasn't slept in and nothing was disturbed. That's what his mom said. And nobody saw him at the movie theater. And the last time I talked to him, he was acting funny. He was talking funny. He scared me, a little.
(Silence. Enter Hilda.)

TRACEY: Oh please. This is just too serious. He's probably spaced out on drugs or something, wandering around the beach.

HILDA: You're talking about Corvette, aren't you?

DONNA: They'll find him dead. You watch. They'll find his body in some patch of woods somewhere, like they always do. We'll see it on the news one night, how they've matched this stinking corpse's jaw to Corvette's dental records or something gross like that. I hate this.

TRACEY: Are you going off the deep end or what?

DONNA: They'll come out of the woods with this scrap of rotten cloth that will look just like what Corvette had on when he disappeared. He was such a sweet guy.

HILDA: Oh please, Donna. He was not a sweet guy. He was a total asshole.

DONNA: My brother says this happened at another high school across town. This guy disappeared like this. And they never found him and they never heard from him. His parents even hired detectives.

TRACEY: Weird.

DONNA: Maybe it's a serial killer. You know?

(Tracey laughs.)

HILDA: Right.

(Enter Thacker and Monty. Monty carries books and his Bible. Thacker has two sodas.)

THACKER: Oh great. It's the three chiclets.

MONTY: Hi, everybody.

TRACEY: *(Sarcastically.)* 'Hi, everybody?' You must be joking.

DONNA: Hi, Monty.

HILDA: Did you guys hear about Corvette? What do you think happened to him? We think he ran away, except for Donna, she thinks he's dead.

(Silence.)

TRACEY: What do you think, Starch? Does the Bible tell you anything?

(Monty shrugs.)

TRACEY: Come on, you can talk, can't you?

THACKER: Leave the guy alone, Tracey, you're such a bitch.

TRACEY: Well, if I'm a bitch what are you?

THACKER: I'm not the one who stands around picking at people all the time. You must have a really shitty love life or something.

TRACEY: I'm just asking a question. Right, Starch? What do you think happened to Corvette? You knew him, right?

MONTY: I met him a couple of times.

TRACEY: So?

MONTY: Anything could have happened.

DONNA: You think he's dead?

MONTY: It doesn't matter what I think.

TRACEY: I'm with you on that one.

THACKER: Fuck, Tracey, you should listen to yourself.

TRACEY: I'm not any worse than anybody else.

THACKER: Yes, you are.

(Thacker and Monty go to another part of the stage and sit down; they are no longer part of the girls' conversation.)

TRACEY: What a self-righteous monkey-face jerk. Like I'm the only who around here who doesn't like Monty. He's a little creep, that's the reason I treat him the way I do. They're both little creeps, Thacker's just taller. *(Notices both Hilda and Donna watching her.)* What are you looking at? Do you think that jerk is right or something? *(Neither friend dares answer.)* There's nothing wrong with my love life, either.
(Exit Tracey, Hilda, and Donna.)

THACKER: Jesus, what a toad of a day. *(Pause.)* You seem kind of quiet. Those girls get to you?

MONTY: Oh, no. I don't care about them. People are always mean like that. Don't you think so?

THACKER: Did kids make fun of you back where you used to go to school?

MONTY: Sure. *(Pause.)* I don't care. Kids make fun of you but it doesn't mean anything.

THACKER: You find a church yet? You said you were looking for a church.

MONTY: No.

THACKER: Is something wrong? You act like you don't want to talk. Are you mad at me or something?

MONTY: No. I'm just tired. My folks were up late last night. And I couldn't get to sleep.

THACKER: Your folks?

MONTY: My mom and dad.

THACKER: That must be one of those things you say in Louisiana.
(Silence.)

MONTY: What happened to that guy, Corvette? *(No answer.)* You knew him pretty good, didn't you?

THACKER: You just think that because you saw me with him that day.

MONTY: It seemed like you knew him.

THACKER: We hung around some. At the mall and the movies. He was okay I guess, but I didn't really like him. We weren't, like, friends or anything. You know?
(Monty nods.)

THACKER: I guess there are a lot of people I hang around with that I don't know whether I really like them or not. *(Pause.)* Corvette was a faggot, did you know that?

MONTY: That's what kids are saying.

THACKER: He didn't try to keep it a secret, except from his parents. I'm not saying anything he wouldn't have told you himself. He was into some dangerous shit, too. He was going down to the bus station and the public toilets and giving blow jobs. Or letting older guys give him blow jobs, or something. You know what a blow job is?

MONTY: The real name for it is fellatio.

THACKER: Right.

MONTY: We had blow jobs in Louisiana.

THACKER: Corvette probably disappeared from one of those places. Like, he went home with some old guy who was sucking his cock and the old guy paid him to stay, or took him somewhere, or something. He's probably in some big old mansion up in the hills, or in Arizona, or something. *(Monty nods.)*

THACKER: You don't believe it, do you? You think he's dead or something.

MONTY: A lot of times people are dead when they disappear.

THACKER: Well, maybe he is. It's too bad though. He was a good kid. *(Rising, preparing to leave.)* Kind of messed up, though.

MONTY: I only saw him that one time, I guess. With you.

THACKER: *(Laughing, uncomfortable.)* Maybe I was the last person to see him alive. What do you think? I mean, besides the person who killed him.
(Enter Donna on another part of the stage.)

THACKER: Listen, I have to meet this guy. Later, okay?

MONTY: You always have to meet somebody.

THACKER: I'm a social force, what can I say?

MONTY: I have to go home soon anyway.

THACKER: Do you walk your brother and sister home every day?

MONTY: Mom goes sometimes. Like today.

THACKER: *(Nodding.)* Great. Well, later. Okay? Don't let any of those bitches make fun of you while I'm gone. Wave your Bible at them or something, okay?

MONTY: Sure.
(Exit Thacker. Donna has been watching them but trying not to appear to watch them. She has also been checking the direction from which she came to make sure her friends are not following. Monty sees her and studies her a short moment. He gathers his books together and stands. He joins her shyly.)

MONTY: Hi.

DONNA: Hi.

MONTY: You're Donna, right?
(Donna nods.)

MONTY: *(As if they had not met before.)* I'm Monty.

DONNA: *(Softly.)* Everybody calls you Starch.

MONTY: But I'm Monty. It's short for Montgomery.

DONNA: That's a good name.

(Silence.)

DONNA: *(Still speaking so softly Monty has a hard time hearing.)* You shouldn't be with Thacker.

MONTY: What?

DONNA: *(Louder.)* You shouldn't hang around with Thacker.

MONTY: Why not? He's nice to me.

DONNA: He'll get you in trouble.

MONTY: You don't even know him, I doubt you ever talked to him.

DONNA: Corvette told me about him. Corvette lived on my street.

MONTY: What did he tell you?

DONNA: You shouldn't hang around with him. That's all. He's not nice like you think he is. You should listen to me, I know what I'm talking about. *(Donna runs away, in the same direction from which she entered. Monty, confused, watches her.)*

MONTY: He's a nice guy.

(Monty stands there watching her as lights go down. Thacker appears on another part of the stage, keeping his eye on Monty. Lights remain low on both as Tracey speaks. Lights rise on Tracey, facing the audience.)

TRACEY: I'm suppose to have some kind of revelation, right? I'm supposed to reveal that I'm really a nice person and I have nice thoughts, I'm supposed to show how sympathetic I am in my deepest, innermost being. I know that's what Hilda did when she got up here. Crap. The truth is, I feel exactly like I said I feel. I don't like the little creep. A lot of times I don't like much of anybody, but especially I don't like Starch. Slithering around school in that cheap tie with that two dollar Bible he carries everywhere. I mean, talk about crap. What kind of act is that? How does he expect anybody to deal with that? I think it sucks, I think he's stupid, or even a moron, like maybe there's something wrong in his brain. I don't care where he's from, my theory is, he would be the same dork wherever he lived. Who needs it? Jesus sucks. The Bible sucks. Most of the people at this school suck. And I don't mind saying so, no matter who's listening. The whole thing is a waste of time anyway. I mean, school is. And maybe the rest of it is, too. Maybe the whole world is a big waste of time, and I'm the only one in it who's mean enough to say so. *(Pause.)* I mean, the guy wears cheap ties and carries this Bible around, all day. Is he some kind of Mormon or something?

(Lights down on Tracey, lights rise on Thacker, who is still watching Monty, keeping himself hidden. Lights also rise on Evan and Marie, seated on a low wall or bench outside their apartment building. Monty heads toward them. After a moment Thacker follows Monty, careful to keep out of sight. When Monty stops, near Evan and Marie, Thacker hangs back but overhears what follows.)

MONTY: Why are you waiting down here? It's suppertime by now.

MARIE: *(Simply.)* We can't go up.

MONTY: Why not?

EVAN: *(Angry.)* You know why not. They're fighting again. He's yelling.

(Silence, as Monty watches a point above their heads, their apartment window.)

MONTY: He didn't hit her?

(Evan shrugs.)

MARIE: We didn't stay up there, we came back down.

MONTY: Did Mama come to get you at school?

EVAN: *(With contempt.)* You know she didn't. When she wasn't there we didn't even wait.

(Monty sits down beside them.)

MONTY: I'll come myself from now on.

EVAN: We don't need you to come for us, we're not little kids, okay?

(Exit Evan, angry. Silence.)

MARIE: He always gets so mad.

MONTY: I know. He can't help it.

MARIE: I like for you to walk us home. Evan always goes too fast.

MONTY: I like to do it.

MARIE: So you won't stop?

MONTY: No, I won't. *(Silence.)* What are they fighting about? Is he drunk?

MARIE: No. But Mama told him she wants to get a job and she went out looking for one today, and he says she's trying to make him feel ashamed because he can't take care of her.

MONTY: Did she find a job?

MARIE: Not yet. But I bet she will.

MONTY: He won't let her.

MARIE: Why not?

MONTY: He just won't.

MARIE: I wish we could go home sometimes. Don't you?

MONTY: We are home. This is home.

MARIE: But I wish we could go home to where we used to live. Sometimes I wish that, anyway.

MONTY: You don't like it here either. Evan hates it.

MARIE: It's okay, sometimes. I guess. I like school. *(Pause.)* But I miss the way things used to be, when we lived in Louisiana. It seemed like I understood things better. Even when Mama and Daddy were having a fight. I had more friends there, or something. Do you think we could ever go back?

MONTY: I don't think we will. *(Pause; looking toward their apartment.)* Maybe things will get better here, and you won't miss your old friends so much. You told me you knew somebody named Candy, you said she was okay.

MARIE: She is.

MONTY: Well, that's a start. *(Pause.)* I guess we better go inside, before Mama gets worried.

(They stand and begin to exit.)

MARIE: Did you make any friends here yet?

MONTY: Oh, sure.

(Lights to black. Marie, Monty, and Thacker exit. Out of silence and blackness comes Corvette's voice over the sounds from the boom boxes, indicating the Street Angels are present.)

CORVETTE: I think they'll find me soon. I'm not buried very deep. *(Pause.)* There were some dogs sniffing around here yesterday. I was afraid the dogs might dig me up, and, you know. Eat me or something. Drag me around. But they went away.

(Lights rise very slowly on Corvette, who is standing to face the audience. He is dead and there are many wounds on his body, cuts and burns. The Angels are on stage too, guarding Corvette. Corvette continues speaking as the lights rise.)

CORVETTE: It's not very comfortable, lying here. The dirt is cold, especially underneath. The dirt on my face gets a little bit warm sometimes and I think it must be daytime, there must be sunlight. But underneath me it's cold, and kind of wet, with things crawling around. *(Pause.)* Maybe you think I shouldn't talk about this, maybe you think you shouldn't have to listen. Kids get killed all the time, what's the big deal? *(Laughs.)* Kids really do get killed all the time. I should know. *(Pause.)* We're supposed to have this happy childhood, right? We're supposed to have loving moms and dads and safe homes and sweet neighborhoods and life is supposed to be clean and nice and everything, all soft rugs and good furniture and nothing bad ever happens, right? That's us. That's who we are. We are the kids, the next generation, and nothing is supposed to touch us. And when we're little our moms and our dads can still talk to us, or, well, not really talk to us but just talk, and we think everything is okay, and fine, and sweet, and nice. All day long everything is nice. But then we get older. Mom and Dad don't like us so much when we're older. When we were little we were reminding them of something, maybe of who they used to be, when they were all safe and little and happy, maybe reminding them of when they were little kids and everything was fine. But then we get older and we don't remind them of anything nice any more, and we start to get sexual and we start to want to drink the same things they drink and we don't need them so much and they don't like that, we don't stay home so much and they don't like that, and the neighborhood doesn't seem so nice and all the people in it don't seem so sweet and all the kids are older and they hang together. *(Pause.)* Anyway. It turns out to be a world where people get killed. Where kids get killed. Like I did. *(Pause.)* I mean, I already knew some kids who got killed before I did. In my neighborhood, in Glendale, these parents had their kids in a day care center and this man walked into the day care center and shot them, every one of them, and their teacher and the woman who made their lunch. She was this Spanish woman who made tacos and stuff and she didn't even speak English but he shot her. It was on the news, you heard about it, everybody heard about it. This guy shot all these kids with a semi-automatic rifle and then he shot himself, and then the police came and took pictures of all the dead kids and took the bodies away and washed away all the blood. They talked to all his friends and his friends all said he was the quiet type, he kept to himself, who knew he was a monster like that? And they talked to his mom and she said he was not a monster, he was so sweet when he was a little kid himself. *(Pause.)* They couldn't put him in jail because he was already dead so pretty soon everybody stopped talking about it except to say that it was horrible, they just couldn't understand it, and when I was alive I never thought about it very much, but now that I've been murdered too, I understand more. That's just the way things are. It's not a nice world, or a sweet world, or a good world. Mom and Dad wish it were nice and sweet and they tried to make it look like that when I was little, so no wonder they got mad at me when I started to find out that part was all a lie. It's a bloody world. It's a mean, nasty, evil world where people eat each other. All the time. *(Pause.)* No wonder parents are so crazy. No wonder kids are so crazy. Trying to pretend like that, with each other. It catches up with you. *(Pause.)* I didn't even tell you how I died, did I? *(Laughing.)* I didn't even tell you who killed me. But you'll find out. *(Angels circle Corvette with the boom boxes. Sounds rise to their highest level. Angels dress Corvette in a costume like theirs. Exit Corvette and two Angels. One Angel remains. Lights rise on Evan and Monty at a park. Monty carries no Bible and wears everyday clothes.)*

EVAN: What did you bring me down here for?

MONTY: This is a place you could play.

EVAN: Here?

MONTY: It's a park. See?

EVAN: Crap, Monty, look at this place. There's garbage everywhere.

MONTY: But there's people playing here. See? Playing softball and volleyball and stuff.

EVAN: I don't know anybody here.

MONTY: Maybe Mama could bring you down here and get you on a team or something.

(Evan simply glares at him; Monty merely pauses.)

MONTY: Or else you could get some kids from school and make a team. Or something.

EVAN: The kids from school don't hang out in the park to play softball. Basketball, maybe.

MONTY: You could play that.

EVAN: I don't think I'm good enough. *(Pause.)* Most of the kids come down here to hang out. They steal beer and stuff. You want me to do that?

MONTY: No.

EVAN: I could sure give that a try.

MONTY: I wish you wouldn't talk like that.

(Evan looks at Monty as if Monty is deformed or crippled in some way.)

MONTY: Anyway, you have to do something besides hanging around on the street at home or getting in fights with Marie.

EVAN: Marie is a little crybaby piece of shit. She's like you, she lives in this ridiculous dream world, like anybody cares what she thinks or what she does. Pretty soon she'll be taking a Bible everywhere, like you do.

MONTY: I don't have a Bible now.

(Evan shrugs. Silence.)

MONTY: When you hit Marie, you're just like Daddy.

EVAN: *(Suddenly furious.)* I am not like him.

MONTY: Yes you are. You're picking on somebody who's weaker than you are. That's exactly what he does.

(For a moment Evan becomes angry enough to hit Monty and moves toward him. Enter Thacker.)

THACKER: Starch, man, I didn't know you hung out here.

EVAN: *(To Monty.)* You better take that back.

MONTY: *(To Evan, in a low tone.)* Stop hitting Marie when you get mad at her and I will. *(To Thacker.)* Hey Thacker. We were taking a walk, me and Evan.

THACKER: This Evan? Your kid brother? *(Sizes them both up.)* You'd never know you came from the same family.

EVAN: I'm not a dork like Monty is.

THACKER: Starch is not a dork. Starch is a great guy. You should appreciate your own brother better than that.

MONTY: You hang around here a lot?

THACKER: I hang around everywhere. Pretty nasty place, this one, right?

MONTY: *(Sobered.)* We never came here before. Mama never let Evan and me come. I thought it would be nice, green-like. You know.

THACKER: It is green. Sort of.

MONTY: But you couldn't play here.

THACKER: Play? *(Snickers.)* You mean, like, hopscotch or jump rope or something?

(Evan is disgusted at his brother when Thacker mocks him.)

MONTY: Some place to play games, like softball and… *(Pause.)* Never mind.

THACKER: This place is for wild stuff, Starch. This place is for finding the real thing, you know. The real deal.

MONTY: You mean drugs.

THACKER: *(Laughing, but gently.)* Yeah. I mean drugs. And other stuff. Like that little patch of woods over there, and the public bathrooms on the other side, by the gate. There's all kinds of action in there. Guys getting with guys and stuff, making money, trade, all kinds of transactions. You know? Even little guys like your brother here, even kids his age. This place is what you call a free market.

MONTY: But these guys here are playing softball and volleyball and there's some guys playing basketball that we saw.

THACKER: Accountants. Lawyers. Bank managers and stock investors. Entertainment industry people. Public servants. Suits. Day people. Those are the ones that play. Except maybe the basketball, but you have to be really good for that in this park.

EVAN: Can you take us around? You seem like you know everything.

MONTY: Hush, Evan.

EVAN: What did I say? I just wanted him to show us where all this stuff is.

MONTY: I don't want to see any of it.

EVAN: Then I'll go by myself.

THACKER: I don't think so, small man. My friend Starch here wouldn't like it. And I like my friend Starch. (*Eyes Monty directly, in challenge, for the first time.*) He's the one I want to show around.

MONTY: (*After a moment in which he simply watches Thacker; to Evan.*) Come on, Evan. We need to get home.

EVAN: I don't want to go home. There's nothing to do there.

MONTY: We're going home anyway.

EVAN: I said I don't want to.

(*Monty takes his arm. Evan pulls away, angrily.*)

EVAN: Why did you bring me here? Why did we come here?

THACKER: Hey, Evanito, calm down.

EVAN: (*To Monty.*) Why did we come here at all? Why didn't we stay at home? I hate it here, I hate it.

MONTY: I know you do. I hate it sometimes too.

(*Monty reaches for Evan's arm again; Evan pulls away. By now Evan's rage has begun to change to tears.*)

EVAN: Stop treating me like a kid. I can't stand it.

(*Exit Evan from the scene; he runs to another part of the stage.*)

THACKER: Tough for the little guy. Right? I mean, this whole moving to the city thing.

MONTY: Yes.

THACKER: Think we should follow him?

MONTY: I will. He's headed home.

THACKER: You sure about that?

(*Monty nods.*)

THACKER: Hey man, it's all right, you know? The kid will be all right.

MONTY: I know.

THACKER: You look like you need some relief.

MONTY: Some what?

THACKER: Relief. Like a tranquilizer. A nice hit of something. You ever do anything like that?

MONTY: No.

THACKER: You need some fun in your life, Starch. I mean, the Bible thing is great, but Jesus drank wine, you know?

MONTY: How do you know?

THACKER: I went to Sunday School, I know the score. Before my dad split, he took me. To church, too. I used to have a Bible, even.

MONTY: Your dad left your mom?

THACKER: Oh sure. Old story. We used to have this big house in Glendale. Now we live in this place off of San Miguel. Greasy neighborhood. My mom can't stand it but she doesn't have any money to move anywhere better. *(Shrugs.)* So what do you say, why don't you and me go find some fun.

MONTY: I need to get home, I guess.

THACKER: You guess?

MONTY: To help my mom. She's not feeling too good.

THACKER: You need to have some fun, that's what you need. You take it all too serious, Starch. You need to loosen up.

MONTY: Maybe I do.

(Thacker's beeper goes off.)

THACKER: Hey, all right. This is my man.

MONTY: Your man?

THACKER: *(More cautious, suddenly.)* A friend of mine. This old guy. He's really up to the minute, you know? He's loaded with money and he likes to throw it around. *(Pause; speaking with a strange air, as if compelled to make this offer, in spit of himself.)* I could take you to meet him, one of these days.

(Monty shrugs.)

THACKER: Sure you don't want to hang out?

MONTY: I need to go.

THACKER: *(Looking around for a telephone.)* All right. I need to get moving, call my man. Later.

MONTY: Did they ever find Corvette? *(Pause.)* I haven't heard anybody talk about him in a while.

THACKER: Why are you asking me?

MONTY: I was wondering. That's all.

THACKER: *(Beginning to exit.)* Who knows? Listen Starch, keep it in the street, all right? And think about that fun stuff. I'd like to take you places, you know? All right?

(Exit Thacker. Monty remains in place as lights go down. Angel moves toward him. Angel speaks to Monty as though Monty can hear.)

ANGEL: We are hanging with the daddy of all things
hanging in the dark with the daddy
shouting and rising and healing everything, while we are waiting

for things to get better, and it makes me mad
it takes so long
hanging with the daddy takes so long
waiting for things to get better takes too much time
hanging in the dark with the daddy
(Monty exits slowly, in darkness. Angel follows him out. Lights rise elsewhere on Evan, facing the audience.)

EVAN: I hate them for bringing us here. I hate Mama as much as I hate Daddy, and I hate Daddy all the time. I hate him when he sits around the house in his stinking tee shirt spilling beer all over everything and throwing up in the toilet. I hate the look in Mama's eyes when I'm at home, I hate the way she hides. This place stinks and she knows it and he knows it and they act like it's going to be different someday but it never will, and they know that too, they know they're lying and we shouldn't have come here, they know it will never get better here, but they won't take us home, I know they won't, they'll just sit here, and Daddy will keep getting drunk all the time because his job stinks and Mama will keep crying because he drinks so much and because we don't have any money, and they'll fight all night and we'll have to listen, me and Monty and Marie, we'll have to lay in that stinking apartment and listen to him screaming at her and her begging him to go to sleep. Begging him not to hit her. I know. Things can never get better here, not for us. And they ought to know it and do something about it, they ought to take us home, but they won't. So I hate them almost as much as I hate this place. It's all I can feel, this ball of hate that's on fire, that's right here inside me all the time. It's all I can feel, till sometimes I wish I could just go away somewhere. Some place where I'd never have to think about anything again.
(Evan comes down from the platform as Marie enters from another direction.)

MARIE: Evan, what's wrong?

EVAN: Leave me alone, okay?

MARIE: Aren't you going to wait for Monty?

EVAN: I don't want to wait.

MARIE: *(Heading toward him.)* Then I'll go with you.

EVAN: No. You stay here. I don't want you hanging around me.
(Evan exits, almost running into Hilda as she enters.)

HILDA: Watch it, you little jerk. *(Seeing Marie.)* Did you see that guy?

MARIE: Yes.

HILDA: Is he your brother or something? I heard him yelling at you.

MARIE: He's always mad like that.

HILDA: He should watch where he's going.

MARIE: I guess.

HILDA: You go to this school?

MARIE: Yes.

HILDA: I used to go here. My little brother goes here now. You waiting for somebody?

MARIE: My brother. He walks me home.

HILDA: Not the guy who just ran out of here.

MARIE: No, my big brother, Monty.

HILDA: So you are Starch's sister. I thought I'd seen you with him.

MARIE: Starch?

HILDA: That's what everybody calls him.

MARIE: Why?

HILDA: Because of the way he dresses, I guess. *(Pause.)* You're dressed pretty normal.

MARIE: Thanks.

HILDA: You like it here?

MARIE: It's okay.

HILDA: I can't imagine moving away from all my friends, like you guys did. It would be really strange.

MARIE: I guess. *(Pause.)* Do you walk your brother home?

HILDA: I drive us. But my mom has the car today.

MARIE: That's nice.

(Silence.)

HILDA: Did Starch always wear ties, and dress like he does, even back where you came from?

MARIE: You mean Monty.

HILDA: Whatever. Did he always wear those ties.

MARIE: Sure.

HILDA: Why?

MARIE: *(Shrugs.)* I don't know.

HILDA: It makes him stick out so much. You know?

MARIE: I guess so. *(Seeing Monty offstage, and standing.)* There he is. I have to go. It was nice to talk to you.

(Marie exits. Hilda watches her walk away with Monty.)

DONNA: It's me now. I'm the one. I have to hurry because Hilda and Tracey are coming soon, but I'm here. I guess I'm praying. You know? I don't guess anybody's there but I'm talking to somebody. We need help. *(Pause.)* You know who I mean. All of us. *(Pause.)* I feel like I really am talking to somebody, like somebody really is there. You know? Do you get that feeling sometimes? That you're speaking in a room where you're absolutely alone except there is somebody with you, invisible. Who hears everything you say. I wish that were true. *(Pause.)* I know things nobody else knows. *(Pause.)* I kept watching Corvette those last few days. I talked to him. I know he's dead now, I know he didn't just run away, and I keep thinking about that last conversation. I talked to him and he seemed like he was burning up with something. He had met somebody. He talked about this man. Just for a minute. This older guy. And when he did his eyes, they were like, I don't know. Like prey. Like he was watching something swoop down on him, and he wanted it. He wasn't scared, but he was hooked on something, not a drug but something else, a feeling. He wouldn't say much, and then he tried to act normal again, and when I asked him a question about this man he just laughed. But I was so scared, because of the look in his eyes. Like he would be killed in the next second and he wanted it. And right then I wondered what his life had been like, to make him feel like that. He had lived on my street forever, he was my neighbor since he was a kid, and all of a sudden I felt like I hardly knew him. And he went away with Thacker and I never saw him again. But when I heard he had disappeared, I knew. *(Pause.)* I never told anybody I talked to him. When I close my eyes I can still see the look on his face. *(Pause.)* It's the way Monty looks, sometimes. Like there's somebody waiting for him, too. *(Pause.)* I know he talks to somebody, when he's alone, I know he's not embarrassed to call it praying, like I am. But he needs it. Somebody's got to help him, if he's going to escape. Somebody.

(Enter Hilda and Tracey.)

TRACEY: *(To Donna.)* What are you doing up there?

DONNA: Nothing. Just thinking.

TRACEY: You look weird. Come on down here, we've got a surprise.

HILDA: You have to see this. *(Holds up an envelope.)* This stuff is unbelievable.

(Donna has joined them by now.)

DONNA: What is it?

HILDA: Dirty pictures. I found them in my uncle Morris's suitcase.

DONNA: Oh, gross.

HILDA: No, you've got to see. Look at this. These are kids. Little girls and little boys.

(Donna takes the pictures as Hilda hands them to her, one by one.)

DONNA: Oh, that's horrible.

TRACEY: I like that one.

DONNA: Who tied her up like that?

TRACEY: Whoever took the picture, I guess.

DONNA: She looks like it hurts. *(Takes another picture.)* Oh, that's horrible. What's that stuff?

HILDA: It looks like grease.

TRACEY: It's probably motor oil. To get him all slick and shiny, you know. You see what he's sitting on?

DONNA: It looks like part of a car.

TRACEY: It is. My brother says it's a crank case and part of an engine. *(Laughs.)* Fun with auto parts. Right?

DONNA: You showed these to your brother?

TRACEY: Sure. He thought they were really neat.

HILDA: Can you believe this stuff? These are all kids our age.

DONNA: Some of them are really young kids.

HILDA: I know. They look like baby Boy Scouts and Campfire Girls.

DONNA: You got these from your uncle? Aren't you afraid he'll find out you took them?

HILDA: You really think he'll tell my mom I stole his pictures of naked little kids? Besides, he'll probably think my brother did it.

DONNA: I'm glad I don't have any uncles who like stuff like this.

TRACEY: Oh please, how do you know you don't?

HILDA: Uncle Morris is okay. I like him because he gives me money for a present. He comes for a visit every couple of years. Dad doesn't like him, he says Uncle Morris is a weirdo. *(Giggles.)* I guess he's right.

(They are silent, each holding pictures, staring at them in fascination.)

DONNA: I wonder where you get pictures like this.

TRACEY: There's clubs for these guys. On the internet and stuff. They have magazines where they put ads about where you can buy junk like this. I bet these pictures cost a lot of money.

DONNA: This guy looks like Corvette.

TRACEY: Oh, you're kidding! Let me see!

(They all study the picture Donna is holding.)

TRACEY: You think maybe it's him?

HILDA: I don't think Corvette was quite that skinny.

TRACEY: You never saw him with his clothes off. Did you?

HILDA: No. *(Pause.)* But this guy's hair is too curly. That's not Corvette.

DONNA: I didn't say it was Corvette, I said it looks like him. And it does. Kind of.

TRACEY: I bet he was into scenes like this. What do you want to bet?

DONNA: What kind of scenes?

TRACEY: Taking off his clothes and taking pictures. So these old guys could look at him.

(Enter Thacker and Monty, talking.)

TRACEY: Hey, Thack. Come look at these.

DONNA: *(Quiet voice.)* Don't call him over here.

TRACEY: *(Waving the pictures at him.)* You know anybody that's into stuff like this?

DONNA: *(Quiet voice.)* Tracey, please don't call him over here.

(Thacker and Monty pause but do not approach the girls.)

THACKER: What kind of stuff you talking about?

TRACEY: Pictures. Dirty pictures.

THACKER: *(Laughing.)* Please Tracey. That's so fourth grade.

TRACEY: You should see these. One of these guys looks like Corvette.

(Thacker reacts to Corvette's name and moves toward the trio. Monty studies Thacker and follows.)

THACKER: What are you talking about?

TRACEY: See? *(Pause.)* Make sure to let Starch get a look.

THACKER: Don't start that crap, Tracey, or we're both out of here.

(Thacker studies the picture that is supposed to be Corvette for a moment, flips through the rest.)

THACKER: That's not Corvette, he was circumcised.

TRACEY: Oh. Well, I guess you would know.

THACKER: Cut the crap, Tracey, I saw him in gym class.

TRACEY: Oh, sure, whatever.

THACKER: Where'd you get this stuff, anyway?

HILDA: They're mine, sort of. I stole them from my uncle.

THACKER: Weird. Look at this kid. I bet she wishes they would untie her. *(Pause.)* No, I don't know anybody who's into this kind of stuff.

TRACEY: Sure you do.

THACKER: These are for old guys who like little kids. Some of these kids are really young, look at this one.

TRACEY: You don't know anybody like that?

THACKER: No way. Those guys are pretty strange. You know, they live alone and don't have any friends. That type. I'd be scared to mess with anybody like that.

HILDA: My uncle used to live with my grandma, but she died. Now he lives alone.

THACKER: See?

TRACEY: I'm disappointed, Thacker, I thought you knew all about the seamy side of life.

THACKER: *(Shrugs.)* Sorry to disappoint you.

DONNA: What about that man Corvette told me about?

(Silence. Thacker is wary.)

TRACEY: What man?

DONNA: Somebody Corvette knew. I talked to him a little while before he disappeared.

HILDA: You never told us that.

DONNA: *(Eyeing Thacker.)* I was scared. But he told me he met this man who liked young guys.

THACKER: So?

DONNA: *(Quietly.)* I thought you knew him, too. This guy, I mean.

THACKER: Did Corvette say that?

DONNA: I can't remember.

THACKER: I don't know who he was talking about.

DONNA: He didn't say much.

THACKER: It was probably some mess he was making up.

TRACEY: This is probably some mess Donna is making up. The whole thing.
(To Donna.) I can't believe you.

MONTY: I don't think Donna would make anything up.

(Everyone is surprised that Monty has spoken.)

TRACEY: What do you know about it?

MONTY: *(Embarrassed.)* Donna doesn't make stuff up. Do you, Donna?

DONNA: No.

HILDA: Oh my God.

TRACEY: This is ridiculous. Donna, you make stuff up all the time.

HILDA: Starch wants Donna for a sweetheart. Look at him.

(Silence. Thacker guides Monty away from the trio.)

THACKER: Come on, Starch, these guys are about to get nasty on you.

TRACEY: Are you serious? Starch and Donna? This is hilarious.

DONNA: Leave him alone, Tracey. Please.

TRACEY: Do you like that little creep?

DONNA: I just want you to leave him alone.

TRACEY: How could you like anybody like that? I am seriously worried, here, Donna.

(The trio begins to exit.)

HILDA: We should get a coke and see if we can bring her to her senses.

TRACEY: I agree. *(To Donna.)* You may need a brain transplant. That could be the only way to save you.

DONNA: Leave me alone, Tracey.

HILDA: Did you give me back all the pictures, Tracey? I want all of them. I'm serious.

(Tracey, Hilda, and Donna exit.)

THACKER: So. Do you like Donna?

MONTY: What? Oh. Yes, she's nice.

THACKER: She's got a good body.

MONTY: I guess so.

THACKER: Don't you think about things like that?

MONTY: Sure. I guess.

THACKER: I thought maybe the Bible kept you from thinking, like, impure thoughts, or something.

MONTY: No. *(Pause.)* At least she talks to me like I'm not some kind of a freak.

THACKER: I sure can't figure out why she hangs out with Tracey.

MONTY: She talked to me about you one day.

THACKER: Oh yeah?

MONTY: She told me I should stay away from you, she said you get people in trouble. *(Pause.)* She said you were dangerous.

THACKER: Did you believe her?

MONTY: *(Shrugs.)* I keep hanging around with you, so I guess I don't.

THACKER: I guess a lot of people think that about me.

(Silence.)

MONTY: Why do you hang around with me?

THACKER: *(Shrugs.)* Who knows?

MONTY: I'm serious. I want to know. Nobody else talks to me, they act like I'm a freak.

THACKER: Maybe that's the reason.

MONTY: What?

THACKER: Maybe I like you because everybody else acts like you're a freak. Maybe you remind me of me.

MONTY: You think you're a freak?

THACKER: Sometimes.

MONTY: I don't.

THACKER: *(Laughing.)* You don't know me very well. *(Pause.)* I don't think you're a freak, though. I think you're okay. But I wonder. *(Pause.)* I wonder if you're real.

MONTY: Real?

THACKER: Sure. I wonder if you're as good as you claim to be, or whether it's just fake.

MONTY: I don't claim to be good.

THACKER: *(Laughing.)* Sure you don't.

MONTY: I don't.

THACKER: Right. That's why you carry that Bible around all the time, that's why you're always praying.

MONTY: I'm not always praying.

THACKER: Come off it, man. I see you. You sit in class and you get this look on your face and you close your eyes, for just a second, and your lips move just a little, and I know what you've been doing. I know you've been praying. And I wonder if it's real, if there's anybody you're talking to up there. And I wonder if you're for real.

MONTY: But that doesn't make me good, to do that.

THACKER: What?

MONTY: It doesn't make you good. *(Pause.)* Maybe I am praying. Maybe. But I'm doing it because I'm afraid.

THACKER: What, you're afraid of going to hell or something?

MONTY: No. I'm afraid of this place. I'm afraid of people like Tracey. Like you, even.

THACKER: We're just normal people. Tracey's kind of strange, I guess. But people around here are just like people where you came from.

MONTY: I was afraid of them, too.

(Thacker laughs quietly.)

MONTY: I was. *(Pause.)* There's a meanness to it that I can't stand. To being alive, I mean. Do you ever think about that? *(Pause.)* It's why I pray. All the time. I ask for protection. I want somebody to protect me, and my mom, and my brother and sister. I want somebody to take care of us. Because I'm scared nobody's going to do that and we're all going to, I don't know. Get hurt.

THACKER: You don't pray for your dad.

MONTY: What?

THACKER: Your dad. You didn't say you pray for him to be protected.

MONTY: I pray for him sometimes.

THACKER: Do you think it works?

MONTY: I don't know. Sometimes it makes me feel better.

THACKER: I don't even know where my dad is, any more. Did I ever tell you that?

MONTY: You told me he left you and your mom.

THACKER: That was a while back. I guess I was still in little kids' school. And for a long time we didn't have any money, my mom and me. It's just my mom and me. And we didn't have any money. Because he left us with this big house to pay for and these two cars. Mom still talks about that. *(Pause.)* I don't tell anybody about this stuff, much.

MONTY: It's all right.

THACKER: I guess.

MONTY: What did your mom do?

THACKER: First, she lost everything. The bank took the house and the cars, one at a time. Like torture, right? *(Pause.)* I was old enough to figure out what was going on. Old enough to look at Mom and know she was close to losing it. To going crazy, you know? Because she never handled money before, Dad did all that. She had a part-time job and she tried to go full-time but by the time she did we were living with my aunt, me and her in this bedroom with my aunt and uncle screaming at her to get her shit together. *(Pause.)* So I couldn't stand that and I started hanging out. You know. At the park, and other places. And I got into stuff. I learned how to make a little money in the park, and other places. *(Pause.)* Mom tried to stop me, to keep me at home, but I wouldn't do anything she said. It was like I hated her. I didn't. But it was like I did. So after a while she stopped, she let me do whatever I wanted. She acted like she didn't know I was staying out all night, or drunk, or whatever. *(Pause.)* We don't live with my aunt and uncle any more. We have this little apartment. I stay there most of the time. But sometimes I stay other places. *(Pause.)* I wish I could pray and feel better. I wish it could have helped me then. *(Silence.)*

MONTY: Maybe it could help.

THACKER: Don't be a sap.

MONTY: Maybe it really could, though. Maybe the thought of somebody being there. Being bigger than you are.

THACKER: *(Laughing.)* You don't know. You really don't know anything.

MONTY: But wouldn't you want it, if it was there? Help, I mean? *(Pause.)* You make it sound like some of the things you do are really bad.

THACKER: They are.

MONTY: You don't hurt people, do you?

THACKER: You don't want to know. All right? *(Thacker's beeper goes off, he reaches for it and reads it.)* Bastard.

MONTY: Who is it?

(Silence.)

THACKER: None of your business.

MONTY: It's that man, isn't it? The one Donna was talking about.

(Silence. Thacker rises, begins to exit.)

THACKER: I've got to call this guy. Okay? I'll be right back, we can talk some more. Okay?

MONTY: Who is he?

THACKER: I told you, you don't need to know.

MONTY: But I do know.

(Thacker halts, listens.)

MONTY: You took Corvette to him, didn't you? You took Corvette to him and he's the reason Corvette disappeared.

(Silence.)

THACKER: I didn't want to. I didn't know. Shit.

MONTY: He's real, isn't he?

THACKER: He's real, all right.

MONTY: That day I saw you with Corvette. You were taking Corvette to him then.

THACKER: No, not that day. Later.

MONTY: And he hurt Corvette. He killed him.

THACKER: I don't know. I really don't. I left.

MONTY: But you think he killed Corvette.

THACKER: I don't know what I think. I don't want to think. *(Pause.)* Shit. This is such shit. *(Pause.)* I have to go.

MONTY: You're going to call him?

THACKER: Sure. *(Shrugs.)* What else?

MONTY: You're going to find somebody else for him? Is that what he wants?

(Thacker shrugs.)

MONTY: Don't do it, don't call him. Don't go, just stay here.

(Thacker shakes his head.)

MONTY: I mean it, stay here. Come home with me, have supper at my house.

THACKER: Supper? *(Laughs.)* It's way too late for supper, Starch.

MONTY: No, it's not.

THACKER: Sure it is. It's too late for almost everything. I'm there already, I'm drowning in this shit.

MONTY: No, you're not. You don't have to be.

THACKER: If I don't call him he'll come after me.

MONTY: You can't keep hurting people. You're not like that. All you have to do is stay here, all you have to do is stop.

THACKER: But I don't want to stop. *(Pause.)* Listen, man, I'll see you around, all right? I'll see you around. Don't say anything about this shit, all right? *(Thacker exits, hurriedly, leaving the scene but not the stage. He goes to a high level and stands with his back to the audience. An Angel enters to face him, standing directly in front of him. Lights down on Monty, who exits.)*

ANGEL: If there is something
if there is maybe a place
if there should be a tree, a rock, a meadow
if there should be an orchard, if there is any peace to be found
I hope you will find it
if there are mountains, an ocean, clean winds blowing
if there is something, if there is any peace
I hope you will find it
(Thacker turns to face the audience. He looks from face-to-face. He wants to speak but there is too much that he is feeling, he can't sort it out. Enter Evan, alone. Thacker watches him. The Angel remains in place.)

THACKER: Oh Jesus. Help me. Somebody help me.
(Evan wanders a little, as if he is searching. Thacker continues to watch him. He is thinking many thoughts, he is resisting something, but in the end he descends toward Evan.)

THACKER: Hey, little man. What's up?

EVAN: I'm looking for Monty and Marie.

THACKER: Marie's your little sister?

EVAN: Yeah. Have you seen her?

THACKER: No, man. No little girls at all. I haven't seen Monty either.
(Silence.)

THACKER: So what are you up to?

EVAN: I have to wait for Marie till she gets here. Mom was supposed to walk us home but she didn't come again. Monty usually comes with us.

THACKER: That big brother stuff, huh? You're this little kid and Monty takes care of you.

EVAN: I guess.

THACKER: You need him to take care of you?
(Evan does not know how to answer this.)

THACKER: You're still like this baby, right? You don't go anywhere by yourself?

EVAN: Marie's the baby, not me.

THACKER: You sure about that?

EVAN: I'm sure.

(Thacker steps close to Evan, lays a hand on his shoulder.)

THACKER: You really sure?

EVAN: Yes.

THACKER: You remember me, don't you?

EVAN: Sure. From the park.

THACKER: You wanted me to show you around.

EVAN: Yeah.

THACKER: You still want that? *(Pause.)* I mean, Monty's not here to stop you. You want to come with me? To the park?

EVAN: What for?

THACKER: Just some fun. That's all. A little bit of fun and then you can go home again, all safe and sound.

EVAN: What kind of fun?

THACKER: You'll find out. But only if you come with me. *(No answer; Thacker laughs.)* Oh well, if you're scared of it, we can just forget it.

EVAN: I'm not scared.

THACKER: Oh, no?

EVAN: There's nothing to be scared of. You're just some kid, like I am.

THACKER: Then you're coming?

EVAN: *(Looking around.)* I don't know, give me a minute.

THACKER: I don't have a minute.

EVAN: I need to wait for Marie.

THACKER: Forget the little sister, man. Monty'll be here in a minute. Carrying that Bible, you know? Little sister will be fine.

EVAN: I don't know.

THACKER: *(Shrugs.)* All right, guy. But I can't wait around here for you to change your mind.

(Thacker begins to exit.)

EVAN: Wait a minute.

(Thacker stops.)

EVAN: I'm coming.

(Evan moves, still hesitant, toward Thacker. Enter Marie.)

MARIE: Hey Evan. Evan. Where are you going?

EVAN: Wait there for Monty. Okay?

MARIE: Who is he? Evan! Who is he?

EVAN: Wait for Monty, like I said. He'll be here in a minute.

MARIE: I don't want to wait here by myself.

EVAN: You have to.

MARIE: *(Screaming, afraid.)* Monty! Monty!

EVAN: Shut up. Stop screaming like that.

MARIE: Monty!

(Thacker and Evan begin to exit again. Thacker lays his arm across Evan's shoulder. Enter Monty.)

MONTY: *(To Thacker.)* What are you doing?

(Silence.)

MONTY: Evan, come back here.

THACKER: You don't have to listen to him, little man. We're just going for a walk.

MONTY: *(To Thacker.)* Don't do this. Please don't.

EVAN: Don't do what? What are you talking about?

MONTY: Come here, Evan. Please. *(To Thacker.)* Let him go.

(Monty and Thacker look at each other for a long time. They have no emotion on their faces but something is being communicated between them. Evan looks from one to the other and, after a moment, understands that he is in danger. Evan moves toward Monty. After a moment, Evan and Marie exit. Monty and Thacker are still watching each other.)

THACKER: All right.

MONTY: Thanks.

THACKER: *(As his beeper goes off again.)* You better get out of here.

MONTY: Are you all right?

THACKER: Just get out of here, Starch. Just get away.

(Sounds begin to rise. Marie and Evan run offstage, but Monty lingers as if he would like to say something. He approaches Thacker but Thacker waves him away. By now sounds are loud, are engulfing everything. Monty turns away finally. Lights rise on Corvette, who stands on the highest level of the stage. An Angel leads Hilda onstage. Donna and Tracey follow. Each occupies a different part of the stage, facing the audience.)

HILDA: I was the one who found him. I'll never forget it. I walked into the room and there he was. I wasn't even looking for him but I found him. I wish it had been Tracey, I wish she had been with me. She should have had to see it, like I did; but I was alone. I guess you remember moments like that, when something big happens, and you're by yourself. Not like when we heard about Corvette, we were all together when we got the news, me and Donna and Tracey. The news about Corvette, I mean, about when they dug him up.

ALL EXCEPT THACKER: Sometimes I feel like the sky

has something in it waiting and watching
over my head like eyes from every direction
Sometimes I feel like the sky is waiting for something
waiting to fall down on me like the future
coming to take me somewhere, but it is only
the sky, there is nothing in it at all
(Enter an Angel with Marie and Evan. They take their places.)

DONNA: It was the same day the police found Corvette's body, everybody was finding things, it was almost funny, I mean. We heard he went to the police, Thacker went, or else he was arrested, that's what Tracey thought, he was arrested and that's when he told everything, because he had to, but Monty said it wasn't true, Monty said he went on his own, Thacker went, because he decided he had to, and I believe Monty.

ALL EXCEPT THACKER: We are all waiting for the future
we don't know why we want it
we are all wishing hard for the future to come
so hard when it gets here we don't know it
when the future comes
we are waiting but we don't know
why
we are confused
(Thacker begins to climb slowly toward Corvette, who stands and waits.)

TRACEY: I heard it was Thacker who told the police where to find him, Corvette I mean, buried in the woods somewhere, not even buried very deep, they hardly had to dig at all, it was just like Donna always said, he was dead. And Thacker told the police because he knew all about it, and I felt sick to my stomach, like I would always be sick, and I didn't know why because it was just what I expected, that Thacker was like that, sick inside, it was just what I thought would happen, that he was hurting people, I'll never forget how it felt, and then Hilda found him and I felt so sorry.

ALL EXCEPT THACKER: The sky is full of something sometimes
when we look up we see it
even our parents see it sometimes
the look in their eyes when they lift their heads
over their heads like eyes from every direction
watching and counting the seconds
afraid of nothing
the sky with nothing to hide and everything waiting

(Enter Monty.)

DONNA: And it was Thacker who knew he was dead the whole time, Corvette I mean, and it was Thacker who named the one who killed him and then it was Thacker Hilda found, I'll never forget it, I guess he couldn't decide what to do after that, after telling the police he knew everything, after they took him to find Corvette, after they dug him up, I mean Corvette, with leaves and blood stuck to his face.

ALL EXCEPT THACKER: Sometimes I feel like crying, I don't know
   why I would do it or where I would sit
   and if somebody found me I don't know what
   I would say, something stupid I guess
   The easiest words I could think of, I'm lonely
   I wish I had someone to talk to
   some days I get so crazy inside
   (Thacker reaches Corvette. He turns to face the audience. Corvette embraces him from behind and they sway gently from side to side.)

HILDA: But I'm the one who found Thacker, I can still see it, he was hanging from the lights in the science classroom, he had tied a cord to the iron beam that holds up the ceiling and the lights, he had stepped off a chair with the cord around his neck, he crapped his pants and wet himself, his face was all puffy and blue, and he was hanging there and swinging a little, and the cord was rubbing on the iron and making this sound, like a baby bird crying, I'll never forget it; I guess he couldn't stand it, I mean, what had happened, the way he helped to kill somebody, Corvette I mean, the way he helped to kill Corvette, because he knew the police would arrest him, I guess, or else he was sorry, I don't know, but I'll never forget it, finding him, Thacker.
   (Hilda stops talking, upset. Tracey quietly crosses to her and holds her hand as Thacker speaks, still embraced by Corvette still swaying slightly.)

THACKER: Sometimes I feel like the sky
   is waiting for something
   over my head like eyes from every direction
   waiting to swoop down on me like the future
   like a bird dropping down with its claws stretched out
   wanting to take me somewhere, but it's only
   the sky, there's nothing in it at all
   (Silence. Monty comes to center stage and faces the audience He is carrying the Bible.)

MONTY: I went with him to the police. He didn't have anybody else. So I walked down there and stayed with him. I was just sitting for a long time. He was like my brother, I guess. Or something. So I went with him. And then I left because it took so long. I had to go home. I told them to tell him that, but maybe they didn't tell him anything. They kept him for a long time. I guess they called his mom, I don't know. And then it was the next day, and we all heard the news, the police had found Corvette where he was buried. And Hilda had found Thacker. *(Pause.)* I wish I had waited longer. I wish I had talked to him. *(Pause.)* Why I carry this. *(Lifting the Bible.)* I don't know. Sometimes I feel like something is watching me, all the time watching me, and waiting for me to forget. But I never forget. I'm always careful. *(Setting the Bible on the floor in front of him.)* It doesn't mean anything, I guess. I mean, if you try to talk about it. It doesn't mean anything at all. I read and I read and the words are right there. I read and I feel better myself but I can't help anybody else. I try. But I can't help anybody at all. *(Steps back from the Bible.)* It's there, if you want it. If it means anything. I'm done with it, now. *(Pause; turns to Thacker, at least partway toward him.)* I miss you, Thacker.

(Lights to black.)

END OF PLAY

ANALIESE

by Lynne Alvarez

From the A.C.T. production of *Analiese,* by Lynne Alvarez.
(from left) Mishi Schueller as *Christian* and Summer Serafin as *Nina.*
Photo by Bob Adler.

ORIGINAL PRODUCTION

Analiese was commissioned and first presented by the Young Conservatory New Plays Program at American Conservatory Theater (Carey Perloff, Artistic Director; Heather Kitchen, Managing Director), San Francisco, California, in July, 1997. It was directed by Craig Slaight; visual designs by Elizabeth Mead; costumes by Callie Floor; dance and movement by Chris Mattison; lighting by James Bock; the assistant director was Kevin Crook. The cast was as follows:

THE TOUCAN	Julia Mattison
ANALIESE	Danya Wachner-Solomon
THE PEACOCK	Chase Oliver
CHRISTIAN	Mishi Schueller
NINA IVERSEN	Summer Serafin
HENNER	Kevin Crook
THE SERVING GIRL	Elizabeth Cole
JARL	Anna Hollenbach
PETER	Jeffrey Condeff
THE DANCERS	Anna Hollenbach
	Kevin Crook
THE GIRL	Elizabeth Cole
THE BOY	Chase Oliver
HANS	Jake Bern
SIGRUN	Anna Hollenbach
CARL	Jeffrey Condeff

PLAYWRIGHT'S NOTE

Before I became obsessed with science fiction as a teenager, I loved fairy tales. I loved the drama, the splendor and the utter cruelty of them: the exotic imagery and magical love they expressed. If there were two hundred books of fairy tales in our local library, then I read all two hundred of them. But only one story has haunted me through adulthood and that is *The Snow Queen* by Hans Christian Andersen. Yes, it has beautiful queens and talking flowers, ice palaces, devils and magic mirrors that distort one's very soul—but it is also a love story and the wild adventure of a young girl who goes out alone in perilous circumstances to find out what has happened to her childhood friend. I loved that story even before I realized that my own life would also be a wild adventure in strange lands with fascinating and dangerous people. Yet in all my years of writing plays, I had never found an occasion to write about what this fairy tale had inspired in me...until Craig Slaight asked me to write a play for young actors.

I had been asked to write "children's plays" in the past and had done so, but I had never been asked to write—not a children's play—but as deep and as provocative a play as I could manage for young trained actors. Not only that—but Craig was part Danish and had just returned from a trip to Denmark—the very place the story was set! This was it. Finally I could explore the Snow Queen story with beautifully talented actors of the proper age and with a director who had an extraordinary sense of stage and of Denmark. The play *Analiese* is the result of our combined effort. It is a completely re-created tale. The characters and situations are quite different, although I continued to set the drama in Denmark. However I moved the characters forward from childhood to adolescence and the play forward to the end of the nineteenth century (when the Swedish playwright August Strindberg was first being performed in Sweden and Denmark), since the Snow Queen was now an actress. A toucan and a peacock at an aviary were added; children drunk on opium. It was exhilarating to combine the old with the new and the young with the experienced in our first production. We had great fun. Now we pass it on to you.

—Lynne Alvarez

DIRECTOR'S NOTE

At one point during a lively discussion with the extraordinary Lynne Alvarez, H.C. Andersen's *The Snow Queen* came bounding in—reminding us both of the ageless pull of Andersen's seemingly simple and innocent story. I was interested in exploring adaptation in our New Plays Program and here was Lynne revealing that she had always been drawn to *The Snow Queen* and its potential as a theater piece. Andersen had been my primer growing up with a Danish parent, so I, too, felt the heavy tug of this story—this Scandinavian world that Andersen offers in such a striking and unsentimental form. Could this be a new adventure for playwright and director? After sharing excitement about the prospects, Lynne and I agreed to take the journey.

Six months later (and after a family trip to meet relatives in Denmark, where I visited Andersen's boyhood home in Odense on the Island of Funen), I met Lynne in New York, she with a beautiful adaptation of *The Snow Queen* in hand. As we contemplated the draft, we both felt that Andersen had worked his magic on us and had, in fact, led us to an altogether original story—one that was infused with elements that were reflected in the austere emotional palette of Andersen's unsentimental view of the world, yet framed in the theatrical language and slant of character that Alvarez so successfully brings to her writing. The two young children that experience the life-trans-formation in Andersen's story became teens in Alvarez's play, grappling with their place on the early edge of adulthood in almost desperate proportions. As Lynne shared with me the bits and pieces of the emerging story, I was excited to see the unique knit of Andersen's magical world and Alvarez's strik-ingly vibrant characters placed in dangerous yet hopeful forward motion.

The final draft of the play was titled *Analiese,* the name of the teenage girl who finds love, loses love, and discovers, after much trial, an altogether different life than she ever could have imagined. In a parallel journey, her young boyfriend, Christian, takes steps toward a defined manhood that opens provincial eyes to both wonder and fear, new possibilities and lost innocence. The two young people seek their own future against a backdrop of contrasting social and physical environments. This was a hearty meal for actors! Our path led us to Denmark in the late nineteenth century (remote to most contemporary Americans, young and old). Astonishing to all of us was how much both history and story have to say to us at the end of the twentieth century. The thumbnail-sized Denmark, and the focus of another period, had offered a unique microcosm of a strangely universal story. Much like the army of nineteenth-century painters who flocked to Skagen, the northernmost tip of Denmark (where Analiese's original journey ends and her new one begins), we were captured by this northern light. We returned to tell our audience what we had seen. *Analiese* was Lynne Alvarez's gift to us…it now belongs to the world.

—*Craig Slaight*

ACTOR'S NOTE

It was great to work with so many older actors in *Analiese.* They were like a second family to me. A lot of teenagers sort of adopted me. I loved working with Craig and Lynne Alvarez. And, I really liked working with Danya. She was really fun. The only problem was in the play we were supposed to be best friends but it's hard to be a friend when you can't speak *(the character of the Toucan does not speak).* The only thing I could do was be silent or squawk. I have so many good memories in that play, like when a feather fell out of my costume the stage crew picked me up and sewed it back on. I really loved to be with the cast and crew of *Analiese,* not to mention being the youngest one there.

—*Julia Mattison* (the Toucan)

ACTOR'S NOTE

I remember our first rehearsal of *Analiese* like it was yesterday. Walking into the dimly lit theater, I had no idea what I was about to experience. This was my first time acting in a premiere of a play. I was used to the process of creating and building a character, but I knew a *new play* would have an added spin to it. I had always heard the direction to "own the character you are portraying." In *Analiese,* this phrase became my reality. I had no previous actors or background information to look to.

The first person I introduced myself to was Lynne Alvarez, the playwright whom I would be working with on this journey. I had read some of Lynne's other work and knew of her amazing talent. I was extremely excited and a little nervous to finally meet Lynne. What if she did not think I was right for the role of Analiese... What then? Would she ask me to leave? Could she fire me? Well, despite my neurotic nervousness, our first read-through went exceptionally well. The script we read was a very rough draft of *Analiese.* I did not realize this until we began reading the first monologue during the read-through, and just when my emotions started to click in and I started to feel the words, I heard a "STOP!" My immediate assumption was that I was fired! Well, Lynne luckily just had an adjustment to a verb tense.

The first two weeks of rehearsal were devoted to reading and working the script that was changing every day. It took me a while to become accustomed to this. At first, I found it very challenging to get a good grasp on the character Analiese. I had always done my primary character research within the scripted lines. In this situation, the script and lines were forever changing. I had to trust myself enough to react off my feeling and intuitions about this character. What I did not realize at that time was that my understanding for this young woman named Analiese, was installing itself within me. I was an active participant in the development of the character. This process, I believe, is unique to working with a playwright in a premiere. Usually an actor has a final script to dig into and dissect. In this situation, the foundation of my character work was almost subconscious. This has taught me to trust my feelings about a character.

Our director, Craig Slaight, was incredibly helpful in this process. He supplied us with chapters and chapters of Danish history and literature. This was the first play that I worked on with Craig. I instantly appreciated his directing style. Craig approaches his work with young actors with complete professionalism. I have found it hard to find directors who take working with young actors seriously. Craig's passion for his work fueled and propelled this project to a very powerful production.

Analiese is a very unique play. First of all, there are hardly any contemporary plays for young adults that are as complex and deep as this play. To me this play is about following your heart and passion. When Analiese finds out that Christian has disappeared, her reaction is not to sit and wallow in her grief but to find him, where ever that may be. Analiese ends up rowing around the Danish coast, through storms, encountering drugged-out children, a boy named Hans, and a woodswoman named Sigrun. Not just any young person could do this without turning back at some point. Analiese is a historical piece. At the turn of the century, woman did not usually do these types of things. I have never read a play that takes place in this time period where a young female has so much strength and power. One of my favorite moments in the play is at the end when Analiese finally finds Christian. He assumes that Analiese, being the little girl who is so in love with him, is here to bring him back home and marry. Analiese responds, "And do you suppose that I'm looking forward to staying home to fold your linen and feed the ducks?" This one quotation shows the progressive, modern values that exist in *Analiese.* I had a great experience playing around with her strength, her young age, mixed with the language and movements of the time period in which this play is set.

—*Danya Wachner-Solomon* (Analiese)

ACTOR'S NOTE

I will never forget my first reading of *Analiese*. The droning hum of BART (*Bay Area Rapid Transit train*) and the incoherent announcements of the conductor dissipated as I dove into the first pages. Even on the page, I could hear the voice of Sigrun, my favorite of the three parts I performed that summer, as she crawled into the space, sniffing her surroundings, and observed something immediately unfamiliar: "Smell. Like flowers." I realized, as I began to speak the words out loud, entering the colorful and well-populated group of BART riders who talk to themselves, that this was a character who spoke her own language; her dialect was hers and hers alone, a motley composite of her travels, her adventures, and her life experiences. As the actor, it was my responsibility to investigate those experiences, to create them and make them real and specific, so that I could create a dialect that was equally unique. The challenge had begun.

I will also never forget the first read-through of *Analiese*. In grandiose terms, I saw the playwright as God, and me as the humble pilgrim—what if I failed on my mission? I realize that Lynne Alvarez doesn't sound like an alias for God, but it was the first time my response to a written script would be judged by the Creator. She sat next to the director with a look of wisdom, expertise, and expectation. I entered with merely a sense of inadequacy. I was stricken by how little I knew of the world of *Analiese,* and how incompletely I would flesh out the skeleton of words the playwright had handed me. I slid into my chair and gazed around the table. Then something significant happened: I found myself at eye level with the writer, the director, and my castmates. I realized that this was not a journey involving a hierarchical God scheme, but one in which each person's role was equally important. We were all responsible for the initiation of a new play into the world of theater within the framework of our specific roles; as the actor, I bore the responsibility of being the first to breathe life into the inchoate character Sigrun, and thereby determine *how much* life she had. My response to Sigrun's unusual speech pattern during the read-through, initial and incomplete, albeit, was significant in Lynne's formation of the character Sigrun. Just as Lynne had given me the first step in my process as an actor, I offered her feedback for her revision process. She used the specific qualities I brought to Sigrun's speech to hone the character, and I used the historical and cultural information about Denmark at the turn of the century presented by the director, as well as information about the artistic formation of the play presented by the playwright, to inform my own character biography.

I watched my character evolve over the course of the two weeks Lynne was with us in rehearsal. Sigrun became more specific, more detailed, and more alive. This evolution was made possible only by the dynamic interaction between the playwright and the player. Characters created with the voices of real people are richer with the marks of life. A close friend and I once saw a professional production of *The Diary of Anne Frank* where Anne was performed by the most flawless teenager on earth. After the production, my friend commented that she wished Anne had had a scar on her cheek, some small sign indicating her humanity, that she actually lived, and breathed, and on occasion, fell down and scratched her face. When the playwright has access to real, living actors while she is developing her characters, the actors leave permanent marks on the characters they play, marks that do not necessarily represent the actor, but more the actor's response to the written text. The characters acquire specificities and qualities that could not have formed in the writer's mind.[1]

The building of character specificity was enhanced by the character work Craig *(Slaight, the director)* assigned the actors. We had to write extensive biographies describing our character's desires, dreams, hopes, and fears, as well as many other psychological characteristics. These interior attributes were then used to inform our outward behavior; as Craig would say: "Football coaches 'block'; I find the behavior which dictates actions." Our interior biographies were also read by the playwright, so the interaction and feedback between the playwright and the player continued on many levels.

By the time the play opened, I entered as Sigrun, crawling on my hands and knees, humming a Danish tune I selected from a recording Craig gave me of traditional turn-of-the-century Danish folk songs, in a costume I had helped to create, speaking a dialect I had formed over the five weeks of rehearsal. I had used the input of the playwright, the director, and my fellow actors, as well as studying films, novels and other cultural emblems as my sources to create a gypsy character, a vagabond whose accent was partly Russian, partly Danish, and totally unique. This decision to create a non-nationally specific dialect was informed by the details Lynne added to the text, such as references to Sigrun's trade involvement with other clans (including Hans and his opium-addicted cohorts), and lack of a stationary *home*. These character traits, developed at the table and in rehearsal, through discussions between the playwright, the director, and the actors, are what made Sigrun the wild, stag liver–eating woman she became. To all who step into her shoes (whatever form they might be), enjoy!

—*Anna Hollenbach* (Sigrun)

1. I observed a wonderful example of this as assistant director the following summer for Daisy Foote's, *When They Speak of Rita* (also included in this volume). In Foote's original draft of the play, Jeannie's (Warren's girlfriend) relationship with Rita (Warren's mother) was essentially innocuous. After the first read-through, however, Daisy was moved by the practical qualities that Caitlin Talbot (the actress playing Jeannie) brought to the character, qualities that challenged Rita's impulsiveness and lack of focus. Daisy returned to the next rehearsal with the initial revisions of Rita and Jeannie's relationship, and by the end of the five-week rehearsal period, Jeannie was arguably the character who presented the biggest threat to Rita; she became the one who turned all of Rita's answers into questions and constantly criticized her passivity.

CAST OF CHARACTERS

THE TOUCAN: Large tropical bird (can be played by a child)
ANALIESE: Girl fourteen to fifteen years old
PEACOCK: Tropical bird (nonspeaking)
CHRISTIAN: Boy sixteen to seventeen years old
NINA IVERSEN: thirty-year-old famous actress
HENNER: Man (nonspeaking)
SERVANT GIRL: (nonspeaking)
JARL: Teenage boy
PETER: Teenage boy
YOUNG GIRL SPIRITUAL WARRIOR: ten years old
YOUNG BOY SPIRITUAL WARRIOR: ten to eleven years old
HANS: Spiritual warrior boy age eighteen
SIGRUN: Robber girl seventeen years old
CARL: twenty-year-old painter
DANCERS: Adult, (nonspeaking)

TIME AND PLACE

All action takes place in Odense, the North Beach of Funen, and in the northern regions of Jutland, Denmark, in 1898.

Analiese

SCENE I

Stage is empty except for a wooden boat with oars center stage. Analiese is rowing with great effort facing the prow. A large Toucan sits on the stern. Analiese is not aware of the bird.

ANALIESE: *(Exhausted.)* Skagen. Skagen. I must reach Skagen. *(She rows more. Her hands hurt.)* Blood. *(She looks at her hands. She pulls the sleeves over her hands and keeps rowing.)* I must reach Skagen. *(Sings to herself breathing hard.)*

"The water is wide, I cannot cross over

And neither have I wings to fly…"

God help me.

Right hand, left hand, right hand, left hand, right hand, left…I can't do it. I can't. To have come so far…so far. It isn't fair. God on High, hear me… *(She stops completely winded and scans her surroundings. She sees the Toucan.)* What? I have lost my mind entirely. What are you doing here? I must be seeing things.

(She starts to rise to touch the Toucan to see if it's real, but the bird opens its wings and flaps as if it is about to fly off. Analiese sits down very slowly.)

ANALIESE: Don't leave.

(The bird sees that Analiese is staying put and settles itself down again.)

ANALIESE: How did you get here, you poor thing? Did you escape? Do you remember me? I saw you in the aviary. You're a Toucan. You come from the jungle. It seems like years and years ago I saw you, but it was only months, wasn't it? Could it have been only months ago? That was the last time I saw Christian too. Oh Toucan, it's cold. What a mistake we've made. So far from home. This is no place to be free. *(Sadly.)* Christian. *(Angry, calling.)* Chriiiss-tiaan! Where are you when I need you? Christian! If only you hadn't met that horrid woman.

(End of scene.)

SCENE II

Analiese steps out of the boat. She is in an aviary in winter. Lots of light, bird calls and songs heard. A peacock struts on one wooden cube. A Toucan sits preening its feathers on another cube of a different height. Analiese is followed by Christian. They both carry heavy winter coats.

ANALIESE: Christian it's so hot. It's like summer. It's wonderful. Here! *(She hands Christian her coat.)* I knew it would be like this. Look—oh there's a peacock. Doesn't he look like a prince? Doesn't he look like he has a hundred eyes on his tail? *(She tries to pet it, but it scurries away. She goes to the peacock which cocks its head at her. She copies his movements.)* Pretty boy. Pretty boy. Hello. Hello. *(The peacock goes to nip her and she jumps back.)* You mean old thing.

CHRISTIAN: *(Is over by the Toucan who regards him solemnly.)* Analiese. Come over here. Look at this bird. What a lordly fellow. I wonder what he is.

ANALIESE: His beak's bigger than his body. If he tried to fly he'd fall over on his face.

CHRISTIAN: I really don't think so, Analiese.

ANALIESE: I know that. I'm not such a child as you think. Christian—this is the best. I'm so glad you brought me.

CHRISTIAN: Just be glad your Grandmother's a good cook and I like to stay on her good side.

ANALIESE: You brought me because you like me.

CHRISTIAN: Who could like a scrawny little chicken like you?

ANALIESE: You used to beg me to marry you every two weeks.

CHRISTIAN: What was I, three years old?

ANALIESE: No. Six.

CHRISTIAN: Here take your coat. I've got my own to carry. *(He goes off to look at the other birds.)*

ANALIESE: You were nicer as a little boy, I'll tell you that.

(A fine lady in furs enters with a gentleman and a maid she hands her furs to without looking.)

NINA: *(Goes to the Toucan. Addresses the gentleman.)* Henner—that's a Toucan. Poor thing so far from home and caught in our endless Danish winter. Do you miss the jungle my pretty one? Flying free in the tree tops with your monkey friends chattering about? *(To anyone who's listening.)* He's sacrificed so much to bring us beauty. It's almost like being an actress.

ANALIESE: But there's a difference, Ma'am.

NINA: Excuse me?

ANALIESE: *(Curtsies.)* The bird was captured. He had no choice whether he should bring us beauty or not.

NINA: Artists have no choice either, my dear. *(To Henner.)* Who is this girl? She's very bold.

(Analiese curtsies. Nina moves off. She appraises Christian. Two teen-age friends rush in and surprise Christian. One punches him in the arm.)

CHRISTIAN: Hey!

JARL: So, you coming sledding or not? We've been waiting for hours.

PETER: You should have seen Jarl acting like an idiot.

JARL: I was not.

PETER: Stupid bugger almost got killed. Hitched his sled to a very dashing sleigh and was whipped under it's runners.

JARL: I planned that. The sleigh was damn fast and I skidded out again.

PETER: You planned that?! *(To Christian.)* So?

CHRISTIAN: Analiese...

ANALIESE: I can't believe you're leaving. Don't you want to see the birds?

PETER: Birds are for babies.

JARL: *(Poking him.)* I wouldn't be so quick to say that. Look who else is here.

PETER: God in Heaven. Isn't that Nina Iversen, the actress?

JARL: It's her or an angel.

ANALIESE: She is beautiful.

CHRISTIAN: Very.

JARL: They say the King was her lover.

CHRISTIAN: Not the King of Denmark?

JARL: No. Sweden. He wasn't the only one either. There were many.

PETER: Ooo-la-la, the things she must know.

JARL: We have to meet her. *(He takes a flower.)* I have just the thing. How do I look?

PETER: *(Grabs the flower and offers it to Christian.)* You're too ugly. Here, Christian. You give it to her. I dare you.

CHRISTIAN: Why don't you do it if you're so keen?

JARL: You look older. You're taller. Go on don't be a bloody coward.

PETER: Or will your little "wife" get mad?

CHRISTIAN: She's not my wife. *(He takes the flower and goes to Nina.)*

ANALIESE: I don't care. Go make a fool of yourself! *(Says to the Toucan.)* Boys are so stupid. If you tease them enough you can make them do anything. They'll jump off a cliff to prove what little men they are.

PETER: And what will girls do—cry?

(Analiese walks away. Now that Christian is next to Nina he is very nervous. Nina is facing away. He clears his throat and gives a little stiff bow.)

NINA: *(Turns toward him, but she addresses Henner.)* Ah, the young man with the golden skin.

CHRISTIAN: You're Miss Nina Iversen, the actress?

NINA: I am. And you?

CHRISTIAN: *(Bowing again.)* Christian Pyndt, Ma'am.

NINA: And that flower you're clutching in your hand, might that be for me?

CHRISTIAN: How idiotic. *(He gives it to her.)* Yes of course it's for you.

NINA: A white rose. Mmmmmm, it's perfect. Look Henner, a white rose, wouldn't you know?

CHRISTIAN: What?

NINA: White roses are my favorite.

CHRISTIAN: No. You're making fun of me.

NINA: You're a lovely boy and this is a lovely gesture.

CHRISTIAN: Then I've offended you somehow.

NINA: No. You've brought back a rush of memories, that's all.

CHRISTIAN: Not very good ones I'm afraid. You don't seem pleased.

NINA: Now, I've made you feel badly. I am sorry. It's just—well I'll confide in you a little bit because you're so forward and so dear. *(She takes him by the arm and takes him aside.)* A gentleman I was very much in love with used to fill my rooms with white roses after every performance at the Royal Theater. You can't imagine how many he sent or how their fragrance used to float through my life in those days as if it were the air itself. I can't smell a white rose without thinking of him.

CHRISTIAN: I see. Then I must apologize.

NINA: Apologize? But why?

CHRISTIAN: One rose can hardly be worth your while.

NINA: No, no, no. I love the rose. I haven't had a single white rose since my friend left. So actually, yours is very precious.

(Christian is pleased and doesn't know where to look.)

NINA: You said your name was…

CHRISTIAN: Christian Pyndt, Ma'am.

NINA: Christian. Here's my card. And this is where I stay when I'm in town. Unfortunately, I'm leaving tonight or I would invite you up for tea.

CHRISTIAN: I should love to come for tea and you should tell me more about your life.

NINA: Yes, we should have a splendid talk. But I'm afraid I must go North.

CHRISTIAN: North? In Winter?

NINA: Yes as far North as I can—almost to Skagen. I have an estate. I call it the Ice Palace. It's so austere and white in winter—so deserted. I love to feel the stripping down of conventional time. The living of this life any life, I imagine, involves great and private pain which we share with no one. At the Ice Palace—the pain trails away. It's not so quiet there or so removed that you can't hear yourself think, or that you would even wish to—but you can hear your heart beat. You're too young to have your store of pain yet. I hope you never do. What you would like are the falcons and the sea eagles and the polar bears and whales!

CHRISTIAN: Absolutely! I'd love to hunt a whale or a bear! Are there wolves?

NINA: Oh yes.

CHRISTIAN: You're so right to go North. No one else ever thinks of it.

NINA: I have an idea. What are you doing now?

CHRISTIAN: This afternoon?

NINA: Yes.

CHRISTIAN: I'm going sledding. Why?

NINA: You go with the boys in the square outside?

CHRISTIAN: Yes we hitch our sleds to the fastest ride. Why?

NINA: *(Looks at Henner and smiles.)* I think I'll bring my sleigh by so I can wave to you. I'll throw you a kiss and embarrass you in front of your friends. *(She laughs, takes Henner's arm and they exit.)*

CHRISTIAN: Oh God. I'll die.

(Peter and Jarl rush up.)

JARL: So? So?

PETER: I can't believe she talked to you that long! What did she say?

(Analiese comes up.)

CHRISTIAN: She gave me her card.

JARL: You fop.

CHRISTIAN: *(Looking at Analiese.)* She's leaving tonight. So I don't think she meant anything by it.

ANALIESE: Let's go. I want to go home.

CHRISTIAN: But you so wanted to come.

ANALIESE: It's only birds and flowers. I've seen those before.

PETER: Tell me every word she said to you.

CHRISTIAN: Analiese.

JARL: She touched your arm. Twice. You lucky dog.

PETER: I can smell her perfume on you.

ANALIESE: Your friends are beastly! They've spoiled everything.

CHRISTIAN: I'll get them away. We'll go sledding and I'll come back for you. Meet me under the clock. I'll only be gone an hour or so.

ANALIESE: Fine.

CHRISTIAN: Now don't cry. It makes your nose all red and ugly.

PETER: Come on, Chris.

JARL: Come on.

(They take him away.)

JARL: Peter's right you do smell like Miss Iversen. If I close my eyes, I might kiss you.

CHRISTIAN: *(He looks at Analiese who is crying. He walks back and hands her his handkerchief.)* Here. I'm only going sledding and you've been pestering me for weeks to bring you here. So enjoy it.

PETER: Mr. Pyndt!

ANALIESE: I wish you were six again. *(She returns the handkerchief.)*

CHRISTIAN: Then you'd be only three. Aren't things much better now if you really think about it?

JARL: I can't stand such tender good-byes.

PETER: They make me sick. Come on or the square will be deserted.

CHRISTIAN: *(To Analiese.)* I must take care of these half-wits. They obviously can't do a thing without me.

JARL: Half-wits? You cretin.

CHRISTIAN: Nit-wits.

(They leave.)

(End of scene.)

SCENE III

Analiese has stopped rowing to rest. The Toucan is cawing. It stops its caw again.

ANALIESE: Oh I agree. I could have killed him. Did he really think I would wait like a good little lamb until he'd had his fun? I left right away. I had to walk. It was nearly dark too. An omnibus passed but I had no money and the horses kicked mud on my coat. I was furious. I never wanted to speak to him again! I cursed him and wished him dead a hundred times, leaving me like that! *(She starts to row and then stops.)* How was I to know he had already disappeared? All the time I cursed him, he was gone. *(She pulls her sleeves down to cover her hands and rows.*) We found his sled the next morning on the river where the ice had broken up. I never saw him again. What penance could I make that would be grievous enough-to punish me for my horrid thoughts? I forced myself to pass the river every day where Christian had died. I put branches on the ice to mark the spot where he had fallen through and sat in this boat until I was so cold it hurt. No one ever came. The boat was abandoned too. There was even water frozen in the bottom. So I sat there every day waiting to see a hand appear or his glove, or his eyeless blue face pressing up suddenly under the ice.

(The Toucan cocks its head and looks at her first with one side and then the other. It searches the boat for food.)

ANALIESE: February, March, April the river woke. The ice was melting. One day I sat in the boat eating some bread and trying to picture Christian's face—but a fearsome angel flashed through my mind in white robes with wings that reached from his shoulders to the ground. His face was stern and grave and suddenly he swung a broad silver sword—I swear I could see the glint of it. Then a rush of water moved the boat. It began to drift.

(The Toucan rubs its beak with his wing.)

ANALIESE: Yes I should have jumped, but a strange calmness overtook me. I felt this certainty that I would join Christian—dead or alive. Two boys passed and yelled to me, but I couldn't hear them. The water in the bottom had melted and I found two oars. Soon the river spread out and brought me to a wide beach. There was the ocean. Fear had caught up with me and I was relieved. I could find my way back to Odense. A big clumsy boy passed carrying two buckets of coal.

(The Toucan caws.)

ANALIESE: I am so thirsty.

(End of scene.)

SCENE IV

Analiese steps out of the boat and approaches the boy carrying coal.

ANALIESE: Excuse me. Could you tell me how I might get back to Odense?
(The boy continues walking and won't look at her, as if he is much younger and afraid.)

ANALIESE: I've done something very stupid and now I must get back. Please stop a moment.

(The boy looks offstage guiltily, puts one bucket down and then the other, and stands waiting like an ox for his next instruction.)

ANALIESE: Can you tell me where I am?

ERIK: *(Looks at her as if she's crazy.)* The beach.

ANALIESE: I know. But what beach?

ERIK: *(Carefully picks up one bucket and then the other.)* I can take you to Jutland.

ANALIESE: That's across the bay.

ERIK: Grandpa Urs is a ferryboat man. When he dies I get his boat. He's not really my Grandpa. My father's head was cracked under a carriage wheel.

ANALIESE: I see.

ERIK: My mother didn't want me because I'm simple. Papa was a drunk. Grandpa Urs likes me cuz I'm his eyes now. He's old.

ANALIESE: Are you going to see Grandpa Urs now?

(Erik starts walking.)

ANALIESE: Can I go with you? Does he go to Odense?

ERIK: Sometimes. I think. He has his ferryboat sixty-eight years. I been going… *(He puts his buckets down and counts laboriously on his fingers.)* …six. Wait. *(He stops again. Takes a small mound out of his pocket. Unwraps it, takes a very small bite out of something and chews it slowly.)* Chocolate.

ANALIESE: Grandpa Urs must be very good to you if he gives you chocolate.

ERIK: *(Looks at her as if she's crazy.)* The rich lady give it to me. If I eat one bite every day, I can make it last to… *(He hands the handkerchief with chocolate to Analiese.)* If I don't eat any…to *(Counts on his fingers.)* Next month. Six months.

ANALIESE: Oh, you got this six months ago?

ERIK: Five. November. Next month will be six. I can count pretty good. Next year I'll get more chocolate because I'm bigger and I can push the others away.

ANALIESE: Why would you push them? Why not just ask?

ERIK: No. Did you ever see a walrus? They smell just like a pig. One tried to tipple our boat. *(Taps his head.)* I threw some fish as far as I could from the boat and the walrus went away after it. Next year—when the lady throws chocolates from her boat—I'll grab some and throw them far away so the other boys go off after them—just like the walrus.

ANALIESE: That's very smart.

ERIK: *(He gives her a big smile.)* Yeah. Give me back my chocolate. *(He takes it.)* In November I go to Odense with Grandpa Urs and the lady with red hair throws chocolates from her boat. She's rich. She doesn't use our boat of course. She goes to…to…Skagen.

ANALIESE: How do you know she goes to Skagen? Did she tell you?

ERIK: I didn't talk to her! *(Looks at her like she's crazy.)* I don't know the woman. I talked to the boy with her. He ran to the boat and knocked me down, then picked me up and cleaned my face. He said they were going to Skagen. He was tall. He gave me his handkerchief. See, I got my chocolate in it. *(He unwraps his chocolate and hands her the handkerchief.)*

ANALIESE: You say the boy went to Skagen? With a woman?

ERIK: Grandpa Urs say she's a woman and then some. He says her hair is the color of the Danish flag.

ANALIESE: Red?

ERIK: Sure. He said he'd salute her anytime.

ANALIESE: The boy was alive?

ERIK: *(Rolls his eyes and sighs.)* Of course.

ANALIESE: Tell me…

ERIK: How could he give me the handkerchief if he was dead?

ANALIESE: Does your Grandpa Urs take his boat to Skagen?

ERIK: We go to Jutland. To…to Glatvid Strand for the seals. The sea's too big at Skagen. Maybe if you had a lot of money Grandpa Urs would make a special trip.

ANALIESE: I have no money.

(Erik stops and puts his buckets down.)

ERIK: Then Grandpa Urs won't take you anywhere.

ANALIESE: Could you help me? Could you sneak me on board?

ERIK: *(Agitated.)* I don't know. Sometimes he hits me. I'm bigger but I let him. I scream too.

ANALIESE: You could hide me.

ERIK: I don't know…

ANALIESE: Like a game. Hide-and-seek. I would hide where Grandpa Urs would never find me.

ERIK: Sure. But I couldn't hide. I have to work. *(Whispers to her.)* Sometimes I hide.

ANALIESE: Yes?

ERIK: I hide in the coal bin. You could hide there too.

ANALIESE: I suppose so.

ERIK: He never goes there. And you know what else? Here. *(He hand her his buckets.)* You can carry the buckets and I'll walk next to you. Grandpa Urs will think it's just me alone. His eyes are bad.

(Analiese starts back toward her boat.)

ERIK: Are you stupid? Where are you going? Grandpa Urs's boat is over this way.

ANALIESE: I must bring my boat and find a way to tie it to the ferry.

ERIK: I'll do that. I'm much stronger than you. I'll tell Grandpa Urs I found the boat and I want it to play in.

ANALIESE: *(Struggling with the buckets.)* Thank you. Thank you kind sir.

ERIK: *(Looks around frantically.)* Sir? Where?

ANALIESE: You. I called you sir.

ERIK: Me? Sir?

ANALIESE: Yes. You've acted like a gentleman. I cannot thank you enough.

ERIK: *(Straightens up.)* My name is Erik. Erik Blid.

(They exit.)

(End of scene.)

SCENE V

Nina's ball. There is only a screen that separates the ballroom from the balcony. Behind the screen we intermittently see couples dancing. We hear music faintly. Christian is out on the balcony in dress clothes.

NINA: Christian, what are you doing out here? Don't you like the music and the dancing?

CHRISTIAN: I think I saw a whale.

NINA: Where? Show me.

CHRISTIAN: There in the bay. Could it have been?

NINA: Yes. Sometimes gray whales wander in to feed.

CHRISTIAN: It was as big as a barn…or a ship!

NINA: You didn't answer my question. Do you hate the dance?

CHRISTIAN: I like it better out here.

NINA: Aren't you cold?

CHRISTIAN: Not at all. I could stay out here forever. Miss Iversen…Nina. I feel there's no limits with you. The world is endless. For all I know there's twice as many stars in the sky.

NINA: That's delightful.

CHRISTIAN: What?

NINA: That you love it here.

CHRISTIAN: I do. There is so much out there I know nothing about.

NINA: And it may be there is much in there *(She points inside.)* that you know nothing about.

CHRISTIAN: Oh. Have I done something stupid? Is everyone talking?

NINA: Would you care?

CHRISTIAN: I want to please you.

NINA: You do.

CHRISTIAN: We did say we'd be great friends.

NINA: We did. And I would be remiss in not pointing out that one does not leave one's friends in the lurch during social occasions. It seems I need a dance partner.

CHRISTIAN: There's at least five men dying to dance with you. Even I could see that.

NINA: Is that why you left?

CHRISTIAN: They have so much more to say to you than I do.

NINA: They certainly think so.

CHRISTIAN: Don't talk down to me. They do. Any wretch can see that. One is a famous surgeon and the other has painted half a dozen naked ladies from Stockholm to Prague—as he continually likes to mention.

NINA: *(Brushing back his hair.)* Christian—what is it?

CHRISTIAN: I think you're the most beautiful woman I've ever seen. There! Do I sound like every other man you've ever met?

NINA: No.

CHRISTIAN: Of course not.

NINA: The men I've met have said it hundreds of times to hundreds of women. I doubt you've ever said it before.

CHRISTIAN: *(Can't look at her.)* Do you think you could arrange for me to go whaling? I want to hunt whales.

NINA: You're such a boy.

CHRISTIAN: Why? Don't ladies want to go and have adventures too? Don't they like to master something, conquer something?

NINA: Yes some of us ladies do, but we don't often want to kill it. And why whales? They lead such obscure and exemplary lives—quite unlike... actresses. And they speak. Did you know? Their voices sound like wind in a cave.

CHRISTIAN: It would please me to go.

NINA: I could arrange it. But it's very brutal. You'd be gone an awfully long time. I would miss you.

CHRISTIAN: At least I wouldn't be leaving here like a thief.

NINA: Ahhhhhh. That's what it is. You're homesick.

CHRISTIAN: I'm not proud of how I left. I stole away like a thief. Poor Analiese must think I'm dead. How could I have done that?

NINA: You did what you had to do at the time. I've found that if you want to make your way in the world, you must be as pitiless as nature. She'll fascinate you one moment, coloring the cliffs black with auks in May and June and then starve half a million to death in August. Sometimes it's for the best.

CHRISTIAN: I hope you're right.

NINA: I'll tell you what. Come dance with me and I'll make sure you become a great hunter. You can track polar bears and wolves and catch all the auks you like and press their little hearts until they die.

CHRISTIAN: You know many hunters then.

NINA: Yes many. Now indulge me. Let's see what your dance master has taught you.
(End of scene.)

SCENE VI

Analiese has gotten out of the boat and is pulling it onto a beach. We hear a stream. The Toucan sits on the prow looking all around. Woods sounds.

ANALIESE: A stream. *(She starts toward it.)* Look. There's a deer. Oh, one antler's broken off. *(She watches the deer leave, which we don't see.)* I wish he weren't afraid of me. He's wiser than I was.
(The Toucan drinks from the stream. Scoops up the water and lifts his head so it slides down his beak into his gullet.)

ANALIESE: *(To the Toucan.)* He's wiser than you too. Trusting strangers. Each person I met I thought was my savior. That was before I learned more about human nature; that you can't rely on people not to feel deeply; or flee or go mad...
(End of scene.)

SCENE VII

As Analiese says the last lines she tugs at the boat. A young girl runs in wildly and begins to spin in circles.

ANALIESE: Girl. Girl. Come help me with this boat.

GIRL: *(Twirling.)* I can't. I'm a lily. I'm a lily. I'm a tiger lily. *(She growls and falls to the ground.)*

ANALIESE: You're spoiled that's what you are.

(The girl doesn't get up. Analiese goes over to her.)

ANALIESE: Girl, are you all right?

GIRL: Listen to the drum—boom, boom!

ANALIESE: Look at you half-naked and there's still snow on the ground. Who let you out like this?

(The girl moans.)

ANALIESE: Are you all right? Should I call your mother?

GIRL: There are only two notes—boom, boom. Hark—the women's dirge. Hark—the cry of priests. The Hindu woman stands on the funeral pyre in her long red robe; the flames fly up around her and her dead husband. But the Hindu woman is thinking of the living man there in the crowd whose eyes burn hotter than the flames that will soon burn her body to ashes.

ANALIESE: You're delirious. Where do you live? What can I do?

(A young boy stumbles in and sits suddenly staring vacantly.)

ANALIESE: Boy! You there! *(She starts toward him.)*

GIRL: Hot! Can the heart's flame perish in the flames of the pyre?

(Analiese goes back to the girl afraid to leave her.)

ANALIESE: You there, boy. Can you help me get this girl home?

(The girl falls asleep.)

ANALIESE: Wake up. You can't sleep. If you sleep in the snow, you'll die! *(She goes to the boy.)* Boy! Boy!

BOY: Leave me alone. *(He sleeps also.)*

ANALIESE: No. Wake up! What is the matter with you two? Are you poisoned?

BOY: I only speak my own story. I am a stork.

ANALIESE: You are mad.

BOY: *(Grasps her wrist suddenly.)* I know the pond where all little human babies lie till the storks fetch them and give them to their parents. Now we shall fly to the pond and fetch a little brother for the boy who threw stones at us.

ANALIESE: Yes of course we shall. *(She looks around desperately for help.)*

BOY: Yes.

ANALIESE: But if the boy threw stones and was bad and wicked—why bring him a baby? Why don't I take you home?

BOY: In the pond is a little dead baby—it has dreamed itself to death. We'll take it to the boy and he'll cry because we have brought him a little dead brother.

(Hans, an older boy runs in.)

HANS: There you are you wicked children. How many times do I have to tell you not to open that...Who are you?

ANALIESE: *(Struggling to get up and curtsy.)* My name's Analiese and...

HANS: Don't bother curtsying. We don't do that here.

ANALIESE: What do you do here? Poison children?

HANS: There's no time to explain. Give me a hand with the girl. I'll take the boy. Follow me.

(They carry the children across the stage.)

ANALIESE: What is your name?

HANS: Hans.

ANALIESE: What's wrong with the children?

HANS: They've been naughty.

ANALIESE: I see.

HANS: But you don't. I'm responsible for them and now I'll be in a lot of trouble.

ANALIESE: Is that all you can think about?

HANS: They'll be all right. This isn't the first time they've gotten into the cookie jar. Here we are. *(Hans lays the boy down and motions for Analiese to do the same with the girl.)* They'll sleep it off.

ANALIESE: What? Cookies?

HANS: Hardly. *(He straightens his clothing and bows.)* Well hello. Thank you for your help.

ANALIESE: May I sit down?

HANS: Yes certainly.

ANALIESE: Is there something to drink? I'm dying of thirst.

HANS: There's cold tea. *(Fetches her a jar.)*

(Analiese gulps it down.)

HANS: You're awfully brown. Aren't ladies still fashionably pale? It's been some time since I've moved in social circles you could say. Actually, you look quite burned. Does it hurt?

ANALIESE: Yes a bit.

HANS: The Elders say cold tea will take away the sting. Just a minute. *(He fetches a rag soaked in tea.)*

ANALIESE: I'm sorry to be such trouble.

HANS: No trouble. Would you like me to...

ANALIESE: No. I'll do it. Thank you. *(She takes the rag and presses it to her face, neck, and arms.)*

HANS: Did you have a shipwreck? Did the rest of your party die?

ANALIESE: *(Shocked.)* No! Why do you ask?

HANS: You seem to be alone. And if you'll pardon me for saying this. You seem to be in terrible condition.

ANALIESE: I'll be fine in a moment. Thank you.

HANS: There's some dried fish if you like.

ANALIESE: More tea please. I won't bother you much longer.

HANS: *(Brings water and watches her closely as she gulps it down.)* You really must stay with us and rest. It will be quite proper. The Elders will be here any minute. I'm sure they'll help you get back to wherever you've come from.

ANALIESE: No thank you. There's someone waiting for me up ahead. He'll be very worried if I don't make it.

HANS: I see. Where is your meeting place?

ANALIESE: Oh. Up near Skagen.

HANS: That's a long ways. Come. You must stay with us. You don't have much strength and you can hardly walk there alone. It's several days journey and although most of the animals you meet seem charming—they're not when you get to know them. Especially wolves. I'd hate to meet one face-to-face. They're fascinating and they look at you like people do. But not good people.

ANALIESE: Wolves?

HANS: Yes. Even the deer will stomp you. Especially if you find one with a baby.

ANALIESE: I wouldn't walk anyway. I have a boat. I'll go along the coast. It's quite serene.

HANS: You don't look very presentable for a meeting.

ANALIESE: Oh yes. The coal bin. I'm filthy.

HANS: You seem to have ripped your dress in several places.

ANALIESE: Where?

HANS: *(Touching her lightly, but they are both very aware of it.)* Here and over here. You must get cold.

ANALIESE: Yes I do.

HANS: We're great weavers here. I know we'll have something to cover it with.

(He exits and comes back with a large homespun brown shawl.) It's a pity, everything we make is brown.

(Again he helps her on with the shawl and they are very aware of each other physically.)

ANALIESE: I really can't keep this…

HANS: Please don't refuse out of any stupid convention of propriety. I detest that. Propriety's one of the few things I'm glad we left behind.

ANALIESE: By "we"—you mean your family?

HANS: Of sorts. "We" are a spiritual community. There's twenty-two of us. All adults except for the wee ones and I. We consider ourselves spiritual warriors foraging for a pure life in the woods. We call ourselves the New Vikings—although we're not the "let's heave rocks and eat brains" variety. And no human sacrifices. Just the occasional bird or horse. In fact, the Elders are down by the river offering horse entrails to Loki, as we speak. Loki is a very tricky fellow and deserves only the best.

ANALIESE: I'm afraid I don't know who Loki is.

HANS: You're a Christian I suppose.

ANALIESE: Yes certainly.

HANS: We were too once. However, now we're true Northmen. We worship the old gods—you must have heard of Thor or Odin, who hung for nine nights from the Tree of the World until he could see the future. Loki is the river god. He acts up in the spring.

ANALIESE: You don't believe in one God?

HANS: The White Christ? Hardly. We're animists with some modern adjustments. You must want to eat now. There's some cold soup I made. I am a good cook, but a dreadful hunter.

ANALIESE: I've imposed enough.

HANS: Didn't I tell you. False modesty is pointless. *(He gets some soup.)* I seem to have a terrible headache. Excuse me. *(He takes two tablets out of his pouch and swallows them quickly.)*

ANALIESE: Aren't you afraid you'll go to Hell if you're not a Christian?

HANS: No we've found something more majestic. We've bridged the idea that on the one hand, God took some dirt and shaped us in his image—you do know that as a Christian no matter how good-looking you are—and I find you reasonably attractive—you're nothing but glorified dirt. And on the other hand God breathed life into you so the essence of God is in you. Those were two halves that didn't fit. How can you be dirt *and* God? The Vikings were right in the first place. You can be dirt and God if God *is* everything—the white birch, the squirrel, the poplar, the sun, the river. To us the whole natural world is sacred.

ANALIESE: I like the way you talk.

HANS: How do I talk?

ANALIESE: Beautiful and complicated.

HANS: Really? I haven't had much practice. It's all been in my head.

ANALIESE: You should be a poet.

HANS: Thank you. That's very kind. I hope to be one. I've read so many poets. I read a tremendous amount. The Elders brought books with them. Hundreds. But I think I've read them all four times by now. My head is full of useful topics—Hindu rituals, the discovery of Africa, the proper construction of meat-drying racks. I read to the children to keep from going mad.

ANALIESE: The children! I'd nearly forgot. You must be worried about them.

(Hans checks.)

ANALIESE: Are they your brother and sister?

HANS: No. No relation.

ANALIESE: And there's no one else near your age?

HANS: No such luck. So actually it's quite nice we stumbled into each other.

ANALIESE: Yes it is. I think you saved my life.

HANS: What kind of person let you travel alone in such dangerous circumstances?

ANALIESE: No one let me. I chose to.

HANS: You ran away.

(Analiese doesn't answer.)

HANS: Let me guess—a young man is involved in this.

ANALIESE: Yes.

HANS: And he's waiting breathlessly for your arrival?

ANALIESE: Yes. Near Skagen, I believe.

HANS: "I believe"? So you're not sure. That means he isn't waiting for you. Is he even expecting you?

ANALIESE: It doesn't matter. I must see if he's there. He might have passed this way last November. You might even have seen him. He was traveling with his…aunt. She has red hair and is very rich.

HANS: His aunt? And her name?

ANALIESE: You wouldn't know it.

HANS: If they pass regularly I might. We trade with travelers all the time.

ANALIESE: It's not important.

HANS: I see. And you're not worried because this young man…

ANALIESE: Christian.

HANS: How fitting. So. You're not worried that Christian's been alone with his red-haired aunt all winter?

ANALIESE: Certainly not.

HANS: Is she ugly then?

ANALIESE: No quite beautiful

HANS: I see.

ANALIESE: Would you stop saying "I see." You don't believe a word I've said.

HANS: There's no sense in worrying. Looks aren't everything. We all have our value. As a friend of mine once said "If only the most beautiful birds could sing, all the woods would be a silent place indeed."

ANALIESE: That's pretty but not very complimentary to me. Will the Elders be here soon?

HANS: I think you need more tea. I'll put a couple of my tablets in it. They're good for what ails you.

ANALIESE: What are they?

HANS: A flower extract. Opium. The British bring it from India. It's quite nice. I've taken some and my head has stopped throbbing. *(Counts them out.)* One, two. That should be enough the first time.

ANALIESE: *(Takes them.)* Thank you.

HANS: It may be a little bitter. I wouldn't mention this to the Elders though. I mean, the pills are harmless. They give you the most amazing dreams. I saw death once. He was a strong old man with a scythe in his hand and great black wings. He was quite friendly. Since then I've lost all fear of death.

ANALIESE: I don't like that you're asking me to lie.

HANS: Not lie. Just keep something back. I can't believe you tell everyone everything that goes on in your life. Otherwise you wouldn't be here.

ANALIESE: You're right.

HANS: Only the Elders are supposed to take these during ceremonies. But I see them sneak a few now and then. They can be quite powerful when you take a lot. We use them to contact our spiritual guides from the past. The Vikings appear to us in dreams and explain their myths.

ANALIESE: Could I have more tea. But no pills.

HANS: Certainly. *(He puts more pills in her tea.)* You seem like such a nice person. It's good to talk to you. However, I have something unpleasant to say. Here's more tea.

ANALIESE: What?

HANS: How to tell you this.

ANALIESE: Just say it!

HANS: A party did come through these woods last November. We were surprised anyone was traveling north at that time. There were two carriages. One had a very lovely red-haired woman traveling with a young man. He had light hair and that golden kind of skin. I remember thinking he was probably a Swede.

ANALIESE: Yes. Yes go on.

HANS: They had a beautiful fur robe thrown over their laps. But then…the wheel on one of the carriages broke as they went over a stream and they were killed.

ANALIESE: It can't be. You're mistaken.

HANS: I'm truly sorry. That's how we got the horses for the sacrifice.

ANALIESE: Oh no! No.

HANS: I am sorry.

ANALIESE: Where are they buried? Take me to see them.

HANS: I'm afraid there was quite a current and they washed out to sea.

ANALIESE: Oh no. Not Christian. Surely not him.

HANS: *(Tries to comfort her awkwardly.)* So you see. You really must stay.

ANALIESE: My beautiful boy.

HANS: There. There. All isn't lost.

ANALIESE: But it is.

HANS: You think so. But you're so young. You could…you can bring so much goodness to the world still.

ANALIESE: I can't think of that.

HANS: So much loveliness. Analiese.

ANALIESE: Hans, please.

HANS: One door is closed, but another opens.

ANALIESE: I must find him.

HANS: If you searched all the beaches of Denmark, how could you possibly find him? If you found anything at all it would only be bones or worse and unrecognizable. Stay here, Analiese. I would be good to you. I would help you through this terrible time and you could save me.

ANALIESE: Hans I hardly know you.

HANS: *(Kneels suddenly and takes her hand.)* Save me.

ANALIESE: Hans, how can I save you?

HANS: Please.

ANALIESE: Save you from what?

HANS: I will dream myself to death. Analiese please. I need your help. I think I'm getting worse. I gave the children opium to keep them quiet while I was dreaming—such gorgeous dreams of color and music. They almost make it bearable here. But I gave the children opium! I gave them too much and they wandered off. What if they had fallen asleep and a wild animal tore them apart? What if they walked into the water and drowned? The worst is I think I would do anything to anyone to keep dreaming. Analiese, stay please. You can have a good life here. You can keep me from harming anyone.

ANALIESE: Could I?

HANS: Yes.

ANALIESE: But Hans, you gave me opium. You said it was harmless.

HANS: I won't do it again. I swear on a thousand stallions, on Thor, on the White Christ if you like. I didn't know how to make you stay, and I needed you to see how seductive it is. How sweet your nerves become, like spun sugar.

ANALIESE: *(Stands up abruptly.)* I must go.

HANS: You can't. It's dangerous.

ANALIESE: Why?

HANS: I …gave you more than you think. Two more pills. Sit down. You must. We can talk tomorrow. It will be clearer tomorrow.
(Analiese sits.)

HANS: Good. Good. Everything will be all right.
(One of the children moans and thrashes about.)

ANALIESE: Hans. Go to the children.

HANS: You will consider it?

ANALIESE: The children need you. The Elders will be back soon.

HANS: Yes. Yes, of course. *(He goes to them.)*
(Analiese bolts out of the door and runs some distance. She stops to catch her breath.)

ANALIESE: Oh God, Christian can you really be dead? *(She sits down shakily. She falls asleep.)*
(End of scene.)

SCENE VIII

Christian and Nina. She is reciting lines to him from Miss Julie *and he is reading another part from a book.*

NINA: You read that very well. Let's go on to the next. *(She turns the pages for him.)* I can't tell you how much help this has been. I'm extremely nervous about this role. We haven't seen a *Miss Julie* for nine years. I must make it mine. She must be imperious yet vulnerable.

CHRISTIAN: I get so caught up with you that I lose my place.

NINA: I wish I could believe you, but you've never been to theater. All right, you're reading Jean, the servant. His girlfriend is asleep in the other room.

CHRISTIAN: We're here?

NINA: Yes, I shall begin. *(As Miss Julie.)* A charming wife she'll make. Does she snore too?

HANS: *(As Jean.)* She doesn't do that, but she talks in her sleep.

NINA: *(Puts down the script.)* How does Jean know Christine talks in her sleep?

CHRISTIAN: He's heard her.

NINA: So you know what is going on there don't you?

CHRISTIAN: What?

NINA: Here where it says they look at each other. There is an understanding between them.

CHRISTIAN: Yes, that he sleeps with her.

NINA: Ah, so you know all about that sort of thing?

CHRISTIAN: Only what I've heard.

(They look at each other.)

NINA: Let's go on then from the look. *(As Miss Julie.)* Why don't you sit?

CHRISTIAN: *(As Jean.)* I wouldn't permit myself to do that in your presence.

NINA: *(As Miss Julie.)* But if I order you to?

CHRISTIAN: *(As Jean.)* Then I shall obey.

NINA: *(Miss Julie.)* Sit then. No, wait. Can you give me something to drink first?

CHRISTIAN: *(Jean.)* I don't know what we have in the icebox. Only beer, I think.

NINA: *(Miss Julie.)* What do you mean, only beer? My taste is very simple. I prefer beer to wine. *(As Nina.)* Try to do the actions as they're written. Hand me a beer.

(Christian mimes giving her a beer.)

NINA: *(As Miss Julie.)* Thank you, won't you have some yourself?

CHRISTIAN: *(Jean.)* I'm not much of a drinker, but if madam orders me—

NINA: *(Miss Julie.)* Orders? Surely you know that a gentleman should never allow a lady to drink alone.

CHRISTIAN: *(Jean.)* That's perfectly true. *(Christian mimes opening a beer.)*

NINA: *(Miss Julie.)* Drink my health now! *(As Nina.)* Hesitate a minute. There. *(As Miss Julie.)* Are you shy?

CHRISTIAN: *(Jean.)* To my mistress's health!

NINA: *(Miss Julie.)* Bravo! Now kiss my shoe and the ceremony is complete. *(Christian starts to do so then pulls back.)*

NINA: *(As Nina.)* Christian, do as it says.
(Christian looks at her then removes her shoe and brings his lips to her foot and kisses it lingeringly. He raises his head and looks at her.)

NINA: Christian, that's not…

CHRISTIAN: I know.

NINA: *(Withdraws her foot slowly.)* You've quite gotten into the role.

CHRISTIAN: The role is me, I think and you.

NINA: You're hardly a servant.

CHRISTIAN: But you're playing with me in all sorts of ways and I understand them all. *(He stands and moves close to her putting his arms around her.)* Just like in the play.

NINA: If things are to change. I must talk to you.

CHRISTIAN: I don't want to talk.

NINA: But you will. Sit.

CHRISTIAN: Am I Jean then? Is that an order?

NINA: Forget the play this is real life and I'm too fond of you to hurt you so we must understand each other.

CHRISTIAN: I told you I understand. You bring a young man here every winter and you "educate" him and then desert him. I've heard the servants and the whispers. Do you think that because I'm young I'm stupid?

NINA: No, but that's a harsh way of putting it. It makes both of us cheap and that is far from true—especially for you.

CHRISTIAN: You say that to all the boys.

NINA: No. To none of them. *(She brushes back her hair.)* I care about you. How do you feel about me?

CHRISTIAN: I can't express it.

NINA: You can do better than that. Tell me what you feel.

CHRISTIAN: You first. Do you feel anything for me?

NINA: I told you I did.

CHRISTIAN: Well what do you think when I'm in the room like this?

NINA: I think…I think your hair is so thick it's like broom bristles. *(She grasps his hair.)* I think that if I buried my fingers in it, it would be like grabbing a horse's mane. Now you. What do you think? What do you feel?

CHRISTIAN: I feel like a wheel of fire is rolling through my chest.

(Nina pulls away.)

NINA: Don't say wild things like that—you could make me fall in love with you.

CHRISTIAN: As much as you were with the man with the roses?

(Nina is silent.)

CHRISTIAN: Was that the King?

NINA: Is that what you've heard?

CHRISTIAN: Yes.

NINA: Don't believe everything you hear, Christian. It was not a great love affair on his part. You may be only seventeen, but it's time you learned some manners. You never, never mention a lady's...other interests unless she brings them up.

CHRISTIAN: You loved him. You're angry.

NINA: I should send you back home. You can sit under your cuckoo clock with your mother and father and eat meatballs and gravy.

CHRISTIAN: No.

NINA: Now you're pouting.

CHRISTIAN: Just don't mention home.

NINA: The mood's spoiled for you, isn't it? But it will come back. Trust me. I'm a romantic idealist, you see. Don't be surprised. I believe with each new lover, I can reinvent myself and dispose of the troublesome person I've become—just like a snake shedding it's skin.

CHRISTIAN: I need some air.

NINA: Go on leave. I'm cross as well.

(Christian exits.)

(End of scene.)

SCENE IX

Analiese in the boat with the Toucan. There is thunder. The Toucan is unsettled and calls out and opens and closes its wings.

ANALIESE: Did you hear that sound? Is it thunder? I hear thunder but there's not a cloud in the sky. *(She listens.)* Thor is the God of Thunder, isn't he? I wonder if Hans is praying to him somewhere. I wonder if it does him any good. He should repulse me. How cruel to put opium in my tea. I had terrible nightmares. In one Christian and I were children again, making peepholes in the frosted windows with heated pennies we pressed against the glass. There was a great snowstorm—the snow fell faster and faster and the flakes were enormous. One became a woman dressed in white lace made up of millions of tiny star-shaped flakes that cut when you touched them. She was so pretty. She was made of ice but she was alive! Her eyes glittered. There was no peace in them. She nodded to us. Christian was wild to open the window. I couldn't stop him and he went out. When he turned to wave, his nose and fingers were black with cold. Does that mean he's really dead? Oh I should hate Hans, but I can't.

(Thunder again. The Toucan flaps its wings.)

ANALIESE: You heard it too. Thunder. It's the end of the world and we'll fall off and be ground to dust. No! I can't think like that. I mustn't give up. Didn't that robber girl appear out of nowhere just when I thought I'd die? *(She steps out of the boat and lies face down.)*

(End of scene.)

SCENE X

A lone figure dragging a large bundle makes its way laboriously to where Analiese has collapsed. Sigrun sniffs around.

SIGRUN: *(Sniffing.)* Flowers! No! *(Sigrun opens her pack and pulls out two sticks of wood. Crosses them and then reacts as if it has become a lighted fire. She sighs, takes off her jacket, warms her hands and her butt. She sits and pulls out a long silver knife from her pack and then something to eat. She eats but sniffs again.)* Yep. Smell. Like flowers. *(She wets her finger and then wets each nostril and sniffs more avidly. She looks around in the snow and comes across Analiese.)* Hey, you! *(She squats looking at Analiese from head to toe. Lifts her head by her hair and lets it drop.)* Still soft. It looks like I shall have a playmate. *(She goes to her pack and takes out a blanket and wraps Analiese in it and gets her in a sitting position. She takes her knife and tests it on her finger.)* Ooooo! Good. Best knife. Poor Russians. *(She watches Analiese for a moment. Analiese is still asleep.)* Look, her little paws are twitching like a dog's when he's dreaming. *(She tickles Analiese's chin with her knife.)* Girl…oh girl. *(Sigrun goes through Analiese's pockets and finds nothing. She shakes her.)* Hey!

ANALIESE: Hans! Don't touch me! Get away!

SIGRUN: Well have it your own way.

ANALIESE: Oh God. *(She looks around wildly.)* Are you the only one here?

SIGRUN: Yep.

ANALIESE: Who are you?

SIGRUN: No name for you. Only my friends know my name. Don't tell me your name either. Knowing stranger's names makes me sad. What if I have to kill you and you have a name. Like killing a pet. Too sad.
(Analiese is shaking violently, recovering from the cold. Sigrun goes in her pack and pulls out some raw meat and sticks it on the end of her knife.)

SIGRUN: You need food. *(She holds the meat over the two sticks as if cooking.)*

ANALIESE: What is that?

SIGRUN: Stag liver. Lucky I gutted a deer this morning. So, are you one of those Viking people? *(She laughs heartily.)*

ANALIESE: Why are you laughing?

SIGRUN: Tell me first. You one of them?

ANALIESE: No. You know them?

SIGRUN: Yep. Sure. I trade with them. *(She holds up her knife.)* I trade them their life for anything they're carrying. But they don't carry much—so I hardly bother them. Ummmmm—maybe sometimes for fun; when they do their ceremonies. *(She laughs again.)* Big, strong Vikings! They dream they're great warriors, but they only sit. They live in their heads. Puh! *(She spits.)* You sure you're not one of them?

ANALIESE: They gave me these clothes. But I'm not carrying anything.

SIGRUN: I know. *(Holds out meat.)* Here.

ANALIESE: No!…thank you.

SIGRUN: Fresh kill.

ANALIESE: No.

SIGRUN: What? You never eat meat?

ANALIESE: Yes, but…

SIGRUN: You don't think about where it comes from. From an animal. Nothing fancy. We're nothing fancy either. *(Sigrun belches.)*
(She eats and Analiese watches hungrily.)

ANALIESE: Maybe I'll have some.
(Sigrun gives her some and laughs heartily. Hans enters wrapped in a blanket. Analiese jumps up afraid.)

ANALIESE: Hans!

SIGRUN: So this is who you were afraid of? Hello Viking boy.

HANS: Don't interfere. I've handled you before.

SIGRUN: Then you were three. Now you're alone.

HANS: *(To Analiese.)* I must talk to you. I must apologize.

SIGRUN: *(To Analiese.)* So?

ANALIESE: Go away Hans. I have nothing to say to you.

HANS: You must let me explain.

SIGRUN: Give me your blanket and you can talk to the girl.
(Hans shoves it at Sigrun.)

SIGRUN: Nice blanket. *(She lays it on the ground and sits watching the two of them as if it were a cock fight.)*

ANALIESE: You could have killed me. Just like the children.

HANS: I never would have left you. I was coming for you. The Elders arrived. I had to wait. Did you see things?

ANALIESE: Bad things.

HANS: You see the power it has? You could lead me away from it. I see that power and more in you.

ANALIESE: If I do have that power, it's one I never wanted and one I don't understand.
(Hans approaches. Analiese backs away. Sigrun is enjoying this.)

HANS: Don't back away. I stopped. See? I would never harm you. But that boy you love. He didn't deserve you. Look how much he's made you suffer; forcing you to travel alone and unprotected through a wilderness.

ANALIESE: He didn't force me. I already told you. I chose to.

HANS: I don't believe you. Love doesn't choose. It happens. It has happened to me.

ANALIESE: Hans.

HANS: With you. You see? You've made me a poet. I wrote you a poem. It's my first. *(He is trembling with cold and emotion.)* "I loved once but not again. Blindly, sullenly completely. I loved a girl not yet a woman. Green eyed as drunk as I was with golden skin and arms that smelled of woods and grass and ached for something as liquid and eternal as love…"

ANALIESE: Hans, just go back to your home. You frighten me.

HANS: Is that all you can say, Analiese?

SIGRUN: Ahhhh. Now I know your name. Analiese.

ANALIESE: Save the poem. It's wonderful. But give it to someone who can love you back. I never can.

HANS: *(To Sigrun.)* She thinks she's in love with a dead man. But I know better. *(To Analiese.)* I know you have deep feelings for me. *(He tries to embrace her.)*
(Sigrun steps in.)

SIGRUN: Are you deaf or crazy? She said she didn't want you.

(Hans looks at her knife, weighing whether he should fight Sigrun or not. He resigns himself to the moment.)

HANS: *(To Analiese.)* This girl is not your friend.

SIGRUN: Yes I am. I've decided. So Analiese, my name is Sigrun. Shall I let him go or kill him.

ANALIESE: Don't harm him. He'll leave. *(To Hans.)* If you love me as you say you do, you will leave.

HANS: All right. *(Backing away.)* You see? I'm gone. I've passed your first test. *(As he is leaving.)* I will see you again, Analiese. *(He exits.)*

ANALIESE: Thank you.

SIGRUN: Sigrun.

ANALIESE: Sigrun.

SIGRUN: So now you know my name.

ANALIESE: I won't forget it.

SIGRUN: But you're leaving?

ANALIESE: Yes.

SIGRUN: After a dead boy?

ANALIESE: I must.

SIGRUN: You have no horse.

ANALIESE: I have a boat.

SIGRUN: So! You should come with me. I'll get you good Russian boots. We'll go rob the Finns. We could become rich. I can show you sights you never dreamed. Bones of whales and polar bears that lie about like the legs and arms of giants!

ANALIESE: I have my own way to go.

SIGRUN: Yep, well, as you like. *(Sigrun lays the blanket out and takes a big loaf of bread from her pack and lays it on the blanket.)*

ANALIESE: What are you doing?

SIGRUN: My pack is too heavy. I have a long way to go. *(She pushes it toward Analiese with her foot.)*
(Analiese takes it.)

ANALIESE: Sigrun—why did you decide to be my friend?

SIGRUN: You're stubborn. You don't complain. I like that.

ANALIESE: Would you have let Hans hurt me, if you hadn't?

SIGRUN: *(Snorts.)* No. Never. I could have sold you to the Turks as a slave. They pay in gold.

ANALIESE: Our paths may cross some time again. *(Analiese exits.)*

SIGRUN: *(She picks up Han's poem. Looks off in direction he left. Crumples paper.)* If you live. *(She waits a beat and then trails Analiese. Her knife is drawn.)*

(Analiese walks to the boat looking carefully around her. Sigrun crouches and watches. Hans enters swiftly intent on Analiese and he does not see Sigrun. Sigrun grabs him around the throat from behind.)

SIGRUN: I knew you would follow.

HANS: Get off me.

SIGRUN: Are you a dunce?

HANS: She needs protection.

(He is fighting her. Sigrun stabs him.)

SIGRUN: Yep, from you!

(He falls with a grunt and is still. Sigrun drags him away.)

SIGRUN: Vikings loved the sea. Go then. The ocean will be your grave.

(She starts to remove her knife. We hear children's laughter and Sigrun leaves, giving the body one last push.)

(End of scene.)

SCENE XI

Analiese and the Toucan. The boat is moving violently.

ANALIESE: The wind! What is this current? Is that the prow of a ship shattered in those rocks? We must throw ourselves out of the boat. But where? And what is this that passes? A swimmer? Hullllooooooo. It's a fish. See he has a silver fin. No look. It's a boy. He has a dagger stuck in his back. He's pitching over. Hans! Hans! Oh he's been killed.

(She tries to reach the body. The boat overturns and she tumbles out clawing her way blindly to shore. The Toucan flies to a rock on higher ground. Analiese drags herself up, coughing water.)

ANALIESE: That was Sigrun's dagger. What has she done?

(The light changes as if the sun is rising. Christian is walking down the beach playful and elated, waving a stick.)

CHRISTIAN: The mighty ocean! I will ride your back to Greenland, to Iceland. I shall see the top of the world. The China seas, Gibraltar and darkest Africa. *(He writes in the sand with a stick.)* This I swear May 5th 1898. Christian Pyndt. *(He bows.)*

(The Toucan flaps its wings.)

CHRISTIAN: *(To the Toucan.)* And you shall be my witness. Strange bird.

(He tries to get close. The Toucan sidles away.)

CHRISTIAN: Come here. Let me look at you. Are you a puffin? Not like any puffin I've ever seen. Well you're not an auk or an eagle or a stork. Come here old fellow. I won't hurt you. What I'd give for a net. You're a pelican. Look at that bill. But those colors—you're the peacock of pelicans. I congratulate you. There…there…easy now. Why don't I just grab you and take you to one of the hunters. They'd know what the devil you are.

(He pounces, but the Toucan flies away.)

CHRISTIAN: Damn.

(The Toucan perches on a rock near Analiese as Christian approaches he catches sight of her.)

CHRISTIAN: Oh hey there! You! help me catch that bird. *(He climbs down to her.)*

(Analiese doesn't answer.)

CHRISTIAN: Hullo…hulloooo…person. Oh! You're a girl. I'm sorry I couldn't tell from up there…

ANALIESE: *(Looks up at him.)* Christian? *(She jumps up and hugs him tightly.)* Christian—have I found you at last!?

CHRISTIAN: *(Pulls her head back so he can looks at her. Amazed.)* Analiese?

ANALIESE: *(Hugging him.)* Where have you been for such a long time?

CHRISTIAN: Analiese. Can it really be you? Here? What are you doing here? How did you find me?

ANALIESE: Hold me. Hold me tight, so I know it's you. Oh Christian you're alive. I thought I should never see you again. *(She bursts into tears.)*

CHRISTIAN: Why are your crying, Analiese? Do I always make you cry then? You must stop. I feel like crying myself. Are you all right?

ANALIESE: I will never be all right. A boy has died because of me. Let me lie down in the sun, with my head in your lap.

(She lies down with her head in his lap. He strokes her hair.)

CHRISTIAN: A boy has died? Who was the boy?

ANALIESE: You don't know him. But he was killed.

CHRISTIAN: How did it happen? Why is it your fault?

(Analiese doesn't answer.)

CHRISTIAN: You've come so far—what has happened to you?

ANALIESE: I don't have words to tell you.

CHRISTIAN: But surely you can! You've always told me all your concerns.

ANALIESE: And you have told me none.

CHRISTIAN: So now, you'll tell me none and punish me for how I left? If this goes on—then we should never speak again.

ANALIESE: *(Singing softly.)* "The water is wide, I cannot cross over..."

CHRISTIAN: Ana, you cannot have come so far just to be a mystery to me. Tell me what has happened to you? How have you come so far to find me?

ANALIESE: *(Dreamily.)* I found a boat and followed the river. I crossed a strait and followed the coast, along the coast to a river, a flood, the ocean. Hans has died because of me. Loving is not so simple as I thought. *(She covers her face with her hands.)*

CHRISTIAN: Hush. Hush. We'll know everything in good time. *(He lifts her up and carries her off.)*

(End of scene.)

SCENE XII

Nina is sitting for a portrait, Carl Lorck sketches rapidly on a large notebook.

CARL: Turn a little to the left. Yes. And lift your chin. Perfect. *(He sketches.)* Do you want tendrils around your face or something more severe?
(Nina is preoccupied, she doesn't answer.)

CARL: Miss Iversen...

NINA: What? Oh—sketch one of each. I'll want several portraits to last the tour.

CARL: You have many admirers.

NINA: That may be, but these are for patrons. Admirers must pay their own painters if they want a portrait.

CARL: Keep your chin up, so your face is toward the light.

NINA: Like this?

CARL: Yes. If you could only bring yourself to smile. Your dimples are very pleasing.

NINA: Wasn't I smiling?

CARL: No you looked rather sad. What were you thinking about?

NINA: Nothing. Whiteness—perhaps you could paint me holding some flowers.

CARL: That's a capital idea. Any particular flower that you'd like?

NINA: Yes. Roses. Make them white. Will you be much longer?

CARL: I want to take advantage of the light. So just a few more minutes.

NINA: That means an hour.

(Christian enters rapidly. He sees Carl and gives a stiff bow.)

CHRISTIAN: Excuse me. I didn't know you were occupied.

NINA: No. Come in. Come in. How is your friend?

CHRISTIAN: I really must talk to you.

NINA: Is she resting comfortably? She must have had an impossible journey.

CHRISTIAN: She's doing well. Thank you for your concern.

NINA: Christian, do you know Carl Lorck?

(They give a slight bow.)

CHRISTIAN: We met briefly last week. On the beach.

CARL: Yes I was painting Mr. Moritz's daughter. It was quite lively. One of his musicians, an American dwarf named Billy, played the violin while Mr. Moritz shot ducks.

CHRISTIAN: May I speak to you alone?

CARL: She really mustn't move. We're at a crucial moment here.

NINA: (To Carl.) Sir?

CARL: All right then. But I can't promise how it will turn out. (He leaves angrily.)

NINA: Artistic temperament. But if one is to have artist friends, one learns to put up with it. Poets are the worst.

CHRISTIAN: So you have a new friend?

NINA: Carl? He's young. I don't think I want any more young friends. Older men are much more grateful.

CHRISTIAN: I'm not ungrateful.

NINA: No? What are you then?

(Christian cannot answer.)

NINA: You really must learn to put a name on your emotions. It makes them manageable—for you and for other people!

CHRISTIAN: Nina, I must take Analiese home.

NINA: Is it duty or desire?

CHRISTIAN: I hardly know. Perhaps there's no difference.

NINA: "The silence before sunrise and tears in my eyes"…is that how the song goes?

CHRISTIAN: I had hoped we'd be friends.

NINA: I see the boy who was my friend fast disappearing. What happened to the great hunter and explorer I shared so many days with? Is he skulking home with his tail between his legs?

CHRISTIAN: Nina…

NINA: I would appreciate it if you called me Miss Iversen in public. Now, I've arranged for your trip back. There will be one horse for the two of you. Maurice the baker will be accompanying you as far as Odense. He must go on to Copenhagen to see his wife, who is pregnant, by him, God willing. You can turn the horse over to Maurice when you arrive.

CHRISTIAN: Thank you. Nina…Miss Iversen…perhaps this is for the best. We are both so different.

NINA: Not so different, Christian. The monogamist and the promiscuous are quite alike when it comes to love. Both are deluded by hope.

(Analiese enters. She has cleaned up but wears the same clothes.)

NINA: Ahhh Analiese…come in.

ANALIESE: *(Curtsies.)* I came to tell you there may be no need for such sad farewells.

CHRISTIAN: It's all been arranged, Analiese. Isn't that so, Miss Iversen?

NINA: Yes. And I hope it will be more comfortable, although less daring, than your journey here.

ANALIESE: That's very generous Miss Iversen, but it may not be necessary. *(To Christian.)* I didn't come to fetch you, Christian—only to find you and make sure you were alive or not. I won't follow you around like a little girl anymore. So you don't have to leave on my account. In fact, I don't want you to. Love is too treacherous a journey for the fainthearted.

CHRISTIAN: I resent that! Just because things aren't simple, doesn't mean I'm a coward!

(Carl steps in and is about to retreat.)

NINA: Carl—have you met Miss Analiese?

CARL: *(Bows.)* Delighted Miss.

NINA: You must help me up. I fear my whole leg is cramped from sitting so long.

(Carl helps her up. She leans against him.)

NINA: Let's take a walk along the beach. The ocean is one of three things that make life worth living.

(As they exit.)

CARL: And pray—what are the other two?

NINA: *(Leaning on his arm.)* Hospitality and revenge.

(Christian and Analiese are both quiet.)

CHRISTIAN: Couldn't you have waited until we were alone to insult me like that?

ANALIESE: Were you two lovers?

CHRISTIAN: No.

ANALIESE: Do you love her still?

CHRISTIAN: We were friends.

ANALIESE: Dear friends.

CHRISTIAN: Yes. She was my dear friend!

ANALIESE: I see.

CHRISTIAN: And Hans?

(Analiese turns away.)

CHRISTIAN: I've been thinking. We should marry before we go back.

ANALIESE: Did I miss something? Was there a proposal?

CHRISTIAN: We can hardly go back to Odense together if we don't marry. In any event, we're of age now.

ANALIESE: I cannot imagine a more reluctant proposal.

CHRISTIAN: I can't help it. You appeared so suddenly. I've just gotten my first taste of adventure and I find it hard to give it up before I even see where it will take me. I have so many dreams. The thought of going home to be the good burgher husband makes me shrivel up inside. But I shall get used to it. I promise.

ANALIESE: And do you suppose I'm looking forward to staying home to fold your linen and feed the ducks? Do you think that knowing a girl who split a deer carcass and then killed a man with the same knife has left me untouched? I wish it had. Then I would never have questioned the difference between love and duty. Now that I do, I don't know what to do with myself.

CHRISTIAN: Do you mean your feelings for me are only of duty?

ANALIESE: The only home I've had all these months has been my feelings for you.

CHRISTIAN: So what are you saying?! You don't care for me any longer?

ANALIESE: I love you Christian.

CHRISTIAN: *(Relieved.)* So what could be wrong?

ANALIESE: I thought nothing of your feelings for me.

CHRISTIAN: But Ana, I love you. Always at the heart of things you've been my life.

ANALIESE: Then how could you leave?!

CHRISTIAN: I never thought of a future without you.

ANALIESE: You put me on a shelf to wait like some porcelain doll that's only played with on holidays! You haven't even kissed me.

(Christian laughs and kisses her. Once lightly. Then he kisses her again passionately.)

CHRISTIAN: Ana, Analiese—what will become of us? I have only a borrowed horse.

ANALIESE: Don't be so solemn. Not yet.

CHRISTIAN: But I have to think about us both. We must have a future.

ANALIESE: Must we decide our whole future at once? Can't we just walk and then walk some more and find some barren place where we can eat by an enormous fire and sleep on the sand?

CHRISTIAN: Like Jacob in the desert?

ANALIESE: Yes.

CHRISTIAN: What good will that do us?

ANALIESE: I don't know! Oh Christian—perhaps if we're lucky—like Jacob— we'll find a stone pillow and when we lay our heads down, perhaps we too can dream of a ladder to heaven.

END OF PLAY

SECOND CLASS

by Brad Slaight

From the A.C.T. production of *Second Class*, by Brad Slaight.
(from left) Lucas Near-Verbrugghe as *Peter* and Malte Frid-Nielsen as *Andrew*.
Photo by Bob Adler.

ORIGINAL PRODUCTION

Second Class was commissioned and first presented by the Young Conservatory New Plays Program at American Conservatory Theater (Carey Perloff, Artistic Director; Heather Kitchen, Managing Director), San Francisco, California, in August, 1997. It was directed by Jack F. Sharrar; Lighting Design and Technical Direction by John Sugden; Scenic Painting by Keith Lewis. The ensemble was as follows:

Julie Bernstein
Asa Kalama
Carin Cymanski
Lucas Near-Verbrugghe
Alex Esteves
Graham Norris
Malte Frid-Nielsen
Sarah Reich
Jenny Gold
Liz Sklar

PLAYWRIGHT'S NOTE

What are the most important learning experiences in high school? Is it the date when the *Magna Carta* was signed, or your first crush? Is it knowing how to find the value of X in an algebra equation, or decorating the gym for the prom? If you're like most people, you realize the most important part of high school is not those fifty-minute segments called "class" it's the memories you have outside the classroom. It's the time spent in the halls, at the dances, waiting for the bus, watching sporting events, or just hanging out with friends. This is where you learn your most valuable lessons—lessons that cannot be, and are not, measured by a report card.

With this in mind I sat down at the computer to bring some of these experiences to life. Like its predecessor, *Class Action* (also developed in A.C.T.'s New Play's program), it would be a compiled script that would allow me the freedom to examine many different experiences, without the structural constraint of making it one complete story. This compendium approach would give me the chance to sample hundreds of voices, rather than just a few. I also decided to make it a continuation of *Class Action*, rather than a sequel. Finally, I wanted the script to work on many levels: It should be insightful, representative of how young people think and feel, relevant to a general audience, and just as important, I wanted it to be entertaining. How's that for pressure?

The first draft yielded over fifty scenes and monologues—almost enough for two plays. My first instinct was to start trimming the tree, but I decided instead to hear the entire script read by the actors. I felt this would give me a chance to hear their voices, get their input, and make a decision from there. The script was then narrowed down to about forty pieces. This was still more than I wanted in the final cut, but since I was familiar with how A.C.T.'s Young Conservatory develops "new plays"—they allow the writer to develop the script with the director and actors—I was confident that we were in good shape to put the scenes up on their feet and narrow the field during the rehearsal process.

Perhaps the most important part of bringing *Second Class* to life was choosing a director who understood the work. My first conversation with Jack Sharrar put all of my fears to rest. Not only did I feel he understood what I was after, I felt an immediate trust in his abilities to help shape my play. I credit the success of *Second Class* to working with him and to the wonderful cast of young actors who were remarkably honest in their approach to the work. Credit must also be given to Craig Slaight, for not only having the vision to create the "new plays" program, but for putting all of the elements together so that my play could develop. When *Second Class* finally opened we had collectively sharpened the focus to thirty scenes and monologues.

Second Class took over a year to evolve from idea to opening night. Looking back at how this all came about I realize that the journey was long, the process was exciting, and the result was a wonderful learning experience, not only for the actors, but also for this writer. My name is listed as playwright, but so many people contributed to what you read. I think that is the true magic of the theater.

—Brad Slaight

DIRECTOR'S NOTE

After reading *Second Class*, Brad Slaight's latest satiric and often poignant depiction of school days, I was more than happy to accept Craig Slaight's invitation to direct his brother's play. Brad had built upon his previously successful *Class Action* (which I had enjoyed greatly), creating new situations and characters that speak to all of us who must go through the multicolored facets of adolescent jubilation and despair, so I looked forward to the collaboration. Directing a play is always a challenging adventure, but when the script is an original property, as with *Second Class*, the adventure is all the more challenging and the greatest of adventures. Fortunately, the Young Conservatory offers a solid support team and a wealth of talent upon which to draw, so there was no problem securing just the right students to create Brad's diverse gallery of characters or creating an appropriate scenic environment. We were also lucky to have Brad with us during the first two weeks of our five-week rehearsal period. This opportunity made final casting of actors in just the right parts, rearranging the collection of scenes to build dramatic impact, and minor rewriting an informative and educational experience for all of us. For instance, with regard to casting, we decided to use more actors than originally called for in the manuscript. This decision not only allowed more students the opportunity to participate, but it helped delineate characters and scenes quite effectively. Throughout early rehearsals Brad, the students, and I continued to work closely exploring the many characters and their relationships to one another in the given circumstances. This discovery work was ongoing and essential to our process. Brad's input and support was constant, even after he had departed. By the time we entered the last week of rehearsals we had shaped his wonderful material into a lively and very human celebration of life.

I can only hope that anyone else who enters the *Second Class* world enjoys the adventure as much as the actors, playwright, technicians, and I did.

—*Jack Sharrar*

ACTOR'S NOTE

I remember first seeing playwright Brad Slaight, and realizing that I would be the one who breathed the first life into his characters. This was the same feeling that I had through the entire process of developing that play: I was part of a creation, that we were bringing into existence—something that no one had ever seen or been a part of before. It was almost like we were giving birth or something, delivering to the world this new and exciting entity. In the past when I had done a play, I felt as if I had to wave my arms frantically trying to search for the meaning and the depth of the words. But with Brad Slaight, the playwright, working with us, we only had to ask and we were given insight into the words, and help in building our characters out of them. And when there were things that we were sure our character would never say, or a *hip* word that seemed a little out of date, Brad listened to us and changed them. It was amazing to be a part of the molding and shaping of a play. Every day we received new versions of the scenes, and sometimes new scenes altogether. We watched the play evolve and take form, until we had developed a final piece.

Second Class was especially great because I was able to play someone my own age. At school I sometimes take on a role twice my age, someone with life experiences that I can never begin to know. But in *Second Class* I played a variety of high school students, people who I could really understand and relate to. I used my own experiences to bring truth and honesty to the characters of trying to make abstract connections between the characters and me. Since *Second Class* is a series of vignettes, each actor played many roles. But each character became a being of its own, with its own personality and its own mind. All of these characters together formed a community, with all of the life and vibrancy that a real high school has.

I would do another new play in a minute. The excitement that comes from being part of the process is like nothing else. It's like constantly having your heart about to beat right out of you. I miss coming to A.C.T. and having an entire new scene to work with. I miss the constant excitement and adrenaline. I miss being part of a cast that is working together to breathe life into a play that no one has ever seen before. And when we performed *Second Class* we all seemed to mesh together to create this new and awesome play with a life unto itself.

—Jenny Gold

CAST

eight students – five female, three male

Optional cast
Because of the number of scenes you can use many more, or even less than the suggested cast.

THE SET

The set can be as simple, or complex, as you wish to make it. You will need only a central playing area and a few benches and chairs or cubes. You may also choose to go with a "two color" set, which reflects your school colors. In the original production they used several painted cubes and two benches. One of the benches was painted such that when stood on end, facing the audience, it looked like a school locker.

MUSIC

You should use transitional music between some of the scenes, as well as sound effects and mood music during some of the scenes.

COSTUMES

Basic school clothes and suggestive props.

TIME AND PLACE

The present. A modern high school.

Second Class

OPEN

As the stage lights come up we hear the sound of loud clock ticking, leading to the sound of a class bell. After the bell there is a single moment of silence followed by the entrance of the student cast, as if they have just been let out of class. We then hear a contemporary rock or techno-pop song. The students talk among themselves. The music fades and Nick breaks away from the group to speak to the audience.

NICK: Last night my Mom asked me what I learned in school. She's been asking me that for ten years and usually I tell her "Lot's of stuff" and she always says "That's nice, honey." But last night I decided to really tell her what I learned. I said, "Mom, in high school the real learning takes place outside the classroom—in the halls, before and after school, hangin' out in the parking lot…and all the other places where we can just be ourselves. That's where we learn about life, love, and how to get along with each other. You see, the things we do outside the classroom will form the foundation on which we build the rest of our lives." There it was. The essence of what I thought high school was all about. My Mom stopped what she was doing, looked straight into my eyes and said, "That's nice, honey."
(Nick crosses back to talk with some friends, most of the Students exit leaving Adam and Jillian….)

SCENE I

JILLIAN and ADAM sit facing the audience.

ADAM: *(DJ voice.)* It's 6:45 on a sunny Thursday morning. The weatherman is calling for temperatures in the high 70s… but that could just be the heat under his cheap toupee. You're listening to KHSR, high school radio. Your school, your music, and your radio station.
JILLIAN: Where it's less talk and more…*(Adam screeches.)* squawk.

ADAM: I'm your host, Madman Adam…along with Jolly Jillian. And now here's something to wake you up to face another day of classes, homework, and the interruption of your good times.

(Adam mimes putting on some music. It's blasting rock music, very loud at first and then fading down to allow for the scene.)

ADAM: What have we got next?

JILLIAN: General announcements…Basketball highlights…and the cafeteria menu for the week.

ADAM: *(Depressed.)* Oh, man…

JILLIAN: What's wrong?

ADAM: No one cares about that stuff, or the music we play…or even this show.

JILLIAN: What's up with you today?

ADAM: We've had this show for six months now and hardly anybody listens to us.

JILLIAN: Lots of kids do.

ADAM: Name three.

JILLIAN: Well, most of the girls on my volleyball team.

ADAM: Great, a bunch of amazons who could kick my butt are my fan base. *(Quick.)* I'm just kidding.

JILLIAN: No, there's some truth to what you say…'cause most of them could kick your butt. *(Pause.)* I think you'd be surprised as to how many people listen. Even though 6 to 8 in the morning is awful early.

ADAM: That's prime drive-time in most radio markets.

JILLIAN: Not that many students drive. And this isn't exactly a market…it's a high school.

ADAM: I just don't know how much longer I can keep doing this.

JILLIAN: I thought we were doing it.

ADAM: Well, you're doing it for extra credit in Drama class. I'm doing it because I'm a serious broadcaster.

JILLIAN: And also you think girls will like you more if they hear you on the air.

ADAM: I've been told I have a sexy voice.

JILLIAN: *(Joking.)* And that you have a face for radio.

ADAM: Thank you.

JILLIAN: Lighten up, Adam. Hey, at least we've gotten to know each other pretty well. You're different than I thought you'd be…in a good way.

ADAM: Really? Well, you turned out different too. I don't usually get along with pretty girls. They're always so into themselves.

JILLIAN: You think I'm pretty?

ADAM: *(Caught.)* Well…uh…sorta.

JILLIAN: That was a very sweet thing to say.

ADAM: I have my moments.

JILLIAN: I didn't think you thought of me that way.

ADAM: What way?

JILLIAN: Like I was a girl.

ADAM: Oh, you're definitely a girl.

> *(They look at each other, perhaps for the first time this way.)*

JILLIAN: Um…We're coming up on one minute.

ADAM: Right. Cue announcements.

> *(Jillian cues up a cart. Adam watches her; the wheels are turning.)*

JILLIAN: Cued and ready.

ADAM: Listen…uh…would you like to go to a movie or somethin' tonight?

JILLIAN: You mean like on a date?

ADAM: *(Quickly.)* We don't need to put a label on it.

JILLIAN: Right…well, in that case I'd love to.

ADAM: You would?

JILLIAN: Yes, I would. *(Looks at watch.)* Ten seconds.

> *(Adam thinks about that and smiles. Jillian counts him down.)*

JILLIAN: And 5-4-3-2- *(Last one is a silent; she points.)*

ADAM: *(DJ voice.)* That was…some loud music! So get up, grab a Pop-Tart, and get your behind on that bus. You're listening to KHSR radio. Your school, your music, and your radio station.

JILLIAN: Where it's less talk and more…*(Adam screeches.)* squawk.

ADAM: *(Pause.)* Usually we make school announcements here, but I thought I'd do something different. Today I thought I'd play a dedication.

JILLIAN: Adam, what are you doing?

> *(He mimes grabbing a cart.)*

ADAM: This next song goes out to a lovely vision, who, like a good pair of glasses, has just come into focus. This dedication is from "Radio Face" to the "Sexy Volleyball Girl."

> *(Adam mimes pushing the music cart in; we hear a contemporary romantic song.)*

JILLIAN: That's my favorite song.

ADAM: I know…

> *(Adam and Jillian look at each other and enjoy the music together for a few moments before the scene ends.)*

SCENE II

Eddy enters; a comet in mid flight.

EDDY: I am Math Man! Super numeric hero and pocket protector of the free
world. Well, maybe that's pushing things. But I do love numbers. All
kinds of numbers. As far as I'm concerned mathematics is the only class
they should teach here. It's got everything you could possibly want. Who
needs English? Math is the universal language. Why teach science?
Everything is made of numbers, not molecules. Take me for
instance…five foot nine inches, 150 pounds, seventeen years old, ten
fingers, ten toes, two arms, two legs, 98.6 degrees! History? Is it not measured in numbered years? Each year contains twelve months, fifty-two
weeks, 365 days, 8760 hours, 525,600 minutes, 31,536,000 seconds. It's
all numbers I tell you. Beautiful numbers. *(Pause.)* Most here think I'm
a lonely guy who has no friends. But that's not true. I'm surrounded by
square roots, logarithms, fractions, positives, negatives, Xs and Ys! I am
no less than, no greater than, but equal to everyone around me. I am
Math man!
*(Eddy exits in a fit of manic joy. He passes Gwen who has entered from stage
right, who spots Kala entering stage left.)*

SCENE III

GWEN: What happened last night?
KALA: Can we talk about it later?
GWEN: Why not now?
KALA: Do you think that's a good idea?
GWEN: Why are you avoiding the issue?
KALA: Why are you pushing me?
GWEN: Don't you think it's better to talk about it?
KALA: Shouldn't we wait until we're alone?
GWEN: Is it really that bad?
KALA: Why do you think I'm so nervous?
GWEN: Why can't you just tell me?
KALA: Do you want to skip out and go somewhere?
GWEN: Where do you think we should go?

KALA: Did you drive today?

GWEN: You want to talk in my car?

KALA: Can you think of a better place?

GWEN: What about our next class?

KALA: Don't you think this is more important?

GWEN: What if we get caught?

KALA: Why are you so paranoid?

   (They start to exit.)

GWEN: Why do I let you talk me into things like this?

   (They are gone.)

SCENE IV

   Jeremy holds a metal "clicker."

JEREMY: My name is Jeremy Polk. I was gonna talk about my experiences in high school these past four years, but my Dad says it's better to show than to tell, so I put together a little slide show.

   (Jeremy clicks the clicker and the lights go out. In the darkness he clicks again. When the lights come back up, we see other members of the cast posed in a frozen tableau behind him representing the picture he describes. The Student playing him in the slides should have glasses on to match the ones that Jeremy wears. Note: Using background music during the blackouts will help cover the time it takes for the cast to reset for the next slide.)

JEREMY: This is Freshman orientation. That's me in the center getting de-pantsed by some upperclassmen. It took me two hours to crawl up the flagpole and retrieve my pants due to the fact that I have very little upper body strength.

   (He clicks the clicker and the lights go out and then come back up showing a new tableau, which represents the slide he will describe.)

JEREMY: That's me in my drivers-ed car...right after the accident. Hey, I swear I didn't even see the tree. Mr. Jamison isn't in the picture because he ran away screaming something about "never again." The two girls that are laughing were wearing their seat belts—the guy on the ground, wasn't. However you'll be happy to know he did recover completely.

   (Clicks again; next slide.)

JEREMY: Here I am at the prom. The mysterious girl you see me with is not from this school. I told everyone her name was Yvette and she was from Paris, France. We went home early that night after she let it slip that her real name was Ethel-Mae and she was my cousin from Paris, Texas.

(Clicks again; next slide.)

JEREMY: This is a shot of a field trip to the Zoo. I'm not in this slide because I missed the bus.

(Clicks again; next slide.)

JEREMY: Here I am being stuffed into someone's locker. It was a tight fit, but they finally got me in.

(Clicks again; next slide.)

JEREMY: Here I am in the science lab just after my experiment blew up. The reason they're holding their noses is because the teacher thought the fumes might be toxic. They weren't.

(Clicks again; next slide...the gang is all girls.)

JEREMY: Here's a shot of me being terrorized by the "59th," a local gang. Notice how I'm pretending to cooperate and be afraid...well, that wasn't pretending. I always thought school was supposed to be a safe place. Guess I thought wrong.

(Clicks again; next slide.)

JEREMY: And finally...Here's me being de-pantsed by some underclassmen. I decided it wasn't worth the bother to try and climb the flagpole this time. As far as I know, my pants are still up there.

(Clicks and when lights come back up he is alone.)

JEREMY: So as you can see, my "Kodak moments" were none too special. Lots of kids say they'll miss all the fun they had in high school. But for me, Jeremy Polk, I can't wait to put some distance between me and this place. I'm told that college will be better. God, I hope so!

(Jeremy exits.)

SCENE V

Lena and Carl enter, holding hands. She sits, he crosses downstage center to address the audience.

CARL: Her name is Lena, and she comes from Sweden. She's an exchange student. I don't know who we exchanged, but we definitely got the better end of the deal. The Bartons are her host family, which makes it hard for me to see her outside of school because I once got caught egging their house on Halloween. *(Pause.)* What's really weird is that after going to this school system since kindergarten, with all the girls that are here, I fall in love with someone from another country. At first I thought it was the mystery of who she was. That she was a secret I had to discover. But I soon learned it was more than that. *(Pause.)* Lena and I try not to talk about what will happen to us when the school year ends, but I know we both think about it quite a bit. Maybe I'll use my college money to buy a ticket and go back with her to Sweden. Or, maybe this is the only time we were meant to have.

(He sits, Lena crosses to the audience.)

LENA: When I come here I was so afraid because the stories we get of your schools are filled with violence. My Fodder wanted me not to come, but my Mudder ruled over him. It is nothing like I expect. American students are much like those in Sweden. You have dreams, yah we do too. I think dreams is what makes us all one people. *(Pause.)* I have boyfriend back home, but there is something special about Carl. At first I think it was mystery of who he was. A secret I had to discover. But I learn that it is more than that. We still have few months togedder before I go back to home. I know this may be all we ever have. So I spend much time with him as I can. I try not to think about leaving America. I try not to think about leaving Carl.

(Carl crosses to Lena and takes her hand; they exit together.)

SCENE VI

We hear the sound of shower water running. Andrew sits on the floor with his back up against a box. He is sobbing. Peter enters and sees him. Andrew tries to cover his tears. Peter mimes turning off a shower knob, the sound of water stops.

PETER: *(Trying to break the tension.)* I think you got it wrong, Drew…you're supposed to take the clothes off before you take a shower.
ANDREW: So you heard? Probably all over school by now.
PETER: Not really. Nathan told me…
ANDREW: He tried to stop them, but he couldn't.
PETER: I know…he told me that, too. You alright?

ANDREW: Yeah.

PETER: Lotta jerks in this school.

ANDREW: I guess it was gonna happen sooner or later. I mean I always waited 'til everyone was done, but Mr. Lawrence knew that I wasn't takin' showers...

PETER: And he just had to tell the guys about it? Well, he's not my Coach anymore.

ANDREW: You don't have to quit the team, Peter. I mean just 'cause you're my brother doesn't mean you gotta side with me.

PETER: Has nothing to do with that, Drew. What they did to you was wrong. And he was wrong for letting it happen.

ANDREW: *(Long pause.)* They saw my scars.

PETER: How could they?

ANDREW: They stripped me before they threw me in here. Then they threw my clothes in after me. One guy said he figured somethin' was up with me 'cause I always wear a long sleeve shirt, even when it's hot.

PETER: Who was it?

ANDREW: It doesn't matter. They all just stared at me. I told 'em about the accident. How the fire just happened so fast and all, but they just kept starin' at my scars, talkin' about how gross I was to look at. A couple of 'em said they was sorry, but they still kept on staring at me.

PETER: I think we should go to the office. We can report Mr. Lawrence.

ANDREW: *(Alarmed.)* No! No, Peter...don't do that! Please... it's just gonna make things worse.

PETER: Okay...that's alright, Drew. If you don't want me to, then I won't. Okay?

ANDREW: Yeah, don't do it.

PETER: I'm not going to. *(Pause.)* Look, I've got some sweatpants in my locker and you can wear my football jersey if you want. Hey, it's even got your name on it.

ANDREW: I just wanna go home.

PETER: You sure?

ANDREW: Yes. Just take me home.

PETER: No problem.

(Peter helps Andrew up.)

PETER: You sure you're alright?

ANDREW: I'm okay.

PETER: That's good.

ANDREW: I'm sorry, Peter.

PETER: What are you sorry about?

ANDREW: 'Cause I know you're gonna hear about it from your friends. Because of me…because you're my brother.

PETER: I can handle myself. And anybody that's stupid enough to make a big deal about somethin' you had no control over…well, sure ain't no friend of mine.

ANDREW: So you're gonna take me home, right Peter?

PETER: Yeah, Drew…I'm gonna take you home.

(Peter and Andrew exit.)

SCENE VII

Annie appears and spots Maria, who sits with a long chain wrapped around her.

ANNIE: They told me you were here, but I had to see this for myself.

MARIA: I know, I promised you a ride home from school.

(Maria reaches in her pocket and tosses Annie some keys.)

MARIA: Drive yourself. I'm gonna be here awhile.

ANNIE: Just what do you think you're doing?

MARIA: What does it look like?

ANNIE: Like you've chained yourself to the cafeteria food locker.

MARIA: It's more than that. This is a protest.

ANNIE: Protest? What, you didn't like the mystery meat they served today? Neither did I, but don't you think this is a little extreme?

MARIA: The cafeteria is just one example of how we are controlled by the state. *(Reads from a piece of paper.)* "We, as students, have no voice in the process that deliberately affects us."

ANNIE: So you want us to decide the menu?

MARIA: And the curriculum, the dress code, the parking policy, the teaching staff, the textbooks, the…

ANNIE: Alright, alright…I get your point.

MARIA: And so will the school board after my protest hits the news.

ANNIE: The news?

MARIA: I sent out a press release to the media—radio, newspapers, TV stations. I'm not going to budge until I got some satisfaction.

ANNIE: You'll budge alright, as soon as Mrs. Benson gets here tomorrow morning and you're stopping her from putting out the daily slop. They don't call her the "Wicked Witch of the Yeast" for nothing. *(Pause.)* What's really going on here?

MARIA: Like I said…a protest.

ANNIE: What if you get expelled? Do you have any idea what that will do to your chances of getting admitted to Harvard?

MARIA: It doesn't matter anymore. They didn't accept me. *(Pause.)* I don't understand it. I've got a 4.0 average. What more do they want?

ANNIE: Who knows? They're a pretty tough school to get into.

MARIA: My Mom's going to freak. *(Off Annie's stare.)* What?

ANNIE: That's what this is all about, isn't it Maria? You're doing this because of your mother.

MARIA: When she was my age she organized several hunger strikes and anti-war protests. She put herself in danger to further the cause of the people, to end suffering.

ANNIE: And now she's a lawyer…she causes suffering. Maria, you don't even want to go to Harvard. That's your Mother's dream.

MARIA: I just want her to respect me…to be proud.

ANNIE: She already should be. 'Cause you've done more and worked harder than anyone I know. God, if I had half your brains.
(Maria thinks about that.)

MARIA: Well, I have worked hard…

ANNIE: Yes you have. And if you want respect, just ask me. 'Cause I respect you. The only one that needs to work harder is your Mom.

MARIA: I don't think I can face her on this one.

ANNIE: How about if I go with you?

MARIA: What?

ANNIE: Don't worry, I'm not gonna tell her off or anything. I'll just be there for moral support. I'll be like a character witness. Her lawyer side will appreciate that.

MARIA: You'd do that for me?

ANNIE: Yes. We'll go over to her office right now. The sooner we tell her, the sooner you can apply to a normal university…maybe even the one I'm going to.
(Maria thinks for a moment. She unlocks the padlock from the chain and slides out of it.)

MARIA: Let's do it now, before I lose my nerve.

ANNIE: On one condition.

MARIA: What's that?

ANNIE: *(Jingles keys.)* I still get to drive your car…I've never driven a Mercedes before.
MARIA: You got it…
(Annie and Maria exit.)

SCENE VIII

Leon enters and looks around as if he hears something.

LEON: If you listen closely…you can hear the past. The voices of my ancestors. My people. *(Pause.)* Most of the kids here call me Leon, but my Indian name is Suyeta [Soo-yay-ta], which means "The Chosen One." I may not look it, but my father is part Cherokee, and my mother has some in her as well. They moved to this area right before I was to start school because they wanted me to be brought up on the land that once was the home of my people. Before the concrete and metal, before the malls and the minimarts, this was all open space. My ancestral tribe lived, hunted, played, and dreamed on this very ground. *(Pause.)* One time I saw an Indian Warrior walking in this hall. His face was painted with bright colors, his clothes made of animal skin, his eyes burned with life. He turned and waved to me, as if to invite me on his journey. *(Pause.)* I don't talk much about this with my friends because they don't understand the ways of my people. They don't understand that my blood flows with such history. But in the quiet moments I feel near to those who came before me. And I have a connection to the past. Their spirit lives on. Even here. Even now.
(He thinks about that for a moment and then exits.)

SCENE IX

An angry Cheryl enters and spots Karen, who is deep in thought; crosses to her and takes her aside in private.

CHERYL: We have to talk.
KAREN: What's your problem?

CHERYL: You're my problem. I can't believe you would just leave that thing in our locker! Do you know how much trouble we could both get in if they saw that?

KAREN: You found it?

CHERYL: It practically fell out on me. Right during break. With teachers walking all over the place. What if they had seen it?

KAREN: It was in a bag.

CHERYL: A paper bag. Real smart, Karen.

KAREN: I just got it this morning…it's not like I was going to leave it in our locker or anything.

CHERYL: Why, Karen? Why do you need…*(Looks around.)* a gun?

KAREN: I have my reasons.

CHERYL: Reasons?

CHERYL: Is somebody after you?

KAREN: Sorta.

CHERYL: Who?

KAREN: I don't want to talk about it.
(Karen crosses and sits, Cheryl follows.)

CHERYL: Well you can talk to me. I'm your best friend.

KAREN: I don't want to get you involved.

CHERYL: You already have.

KAREN: I don't think there's anything you can do.

CHERYL: Well, maybe not. But I have a lot of pull with the front office… you know that. We can really fix the kid who's terrorizing you.

KAREN: That's not going to help. He doesn't go to this school.

CHERYL: What school does he go to?

KAREN: He doesn't go to any school. *(Pause.)* He lives in my house.

CHERYL: Your house? *(Pause.)* Jerry? Your Stepfather?

KAREN: Yes.

CHERYL: I thought you said he's a nice guy.

KAREN: I thought he was.

CHERYL: Jekyll and Hyde, huh? What happened? Bad temper? Did he snap? *(Pause.)* Did he hit you?

KAREN: No…it's not like that.

CHERYL: Well, then what's the problem. I mean, if he didn't hit you then what… *(Suddenly realizes.)* Oh my God…Karen. He didn't.

KAREN: Not yet. But it's gonna be soon. I can tell. Every time he pushes things a little further. *(Pause.)* It started out with little looks and comments. Then last night we were sitting on the couch watching a movie and he kept moving closer to me. I mean, Mom was in the basement doing laundry…she was in the house!

CHERYL: Are you sure about this?

KAREN: Oh, I'm sure alright. I could see it in his eyes. And that little smile of his. Then he started rubbing my leg. I couldn't believe it. He makes me sick. *(Pause.)* It's just a matter of time. Maybe when Mom goes away next week. Or one day he might come home from work early. *(Pause.)* Well, I tell you something…he's in for a big surprise. A really big surprise.

CHERYL: You can't just shoot the guy.

KAREN: Why not?

CHERYL: There's other things you can do.

KAREN: Like what?

CHERYL: Well…*(Thinks.)* I don't know, Karen. I'm not a counselor or anything. But I am your friend. We'll find out what you can do before this thing gets out of hand. We won't let it happen. I swear, we'll get you some help.

KAREN: I'm scared.

CHERYL: I know. But a gun is not the answer. Even though the guy probably deserves it.

KAREN: Yeah, well…there's no bullets.

CHERYL: What?

KAREN: I bought the gun, but I didn't buy any bullets. I just wanted to be prepared. You know, if he tried something I could scare the hell out of him.

CHERYL: That makes sense.

KAREN: I don't really think I could shoot anybody.

CHERYL: You're not going to have to. Come on…let's go see what we can do.

KAREN: I don't know, Cher. My Mom doesn't have any idea. She thinks he's perfect. She's not going to believe me…

CHERYL: Then that's her problem. I believe you. And I know others will too.

(Karen hesitates for a moment.)

CHERYL: It'll be okay.

(Karen thinks for a moment and then decides to go with Cheryl. They exit.)

SCENE X

Mark sits on a cube; he is very intense.

MARK: Eleven o'clock in the morning. A cold sweat came over me as I
looked down at my S.A.T. exam. All around me were hundreds of other
nervous souls, completely at the mercy of this test. Like penguins stuck
on a floating chunk of ice! The Test Monitors stood at the front of the
room, with their roving surveillance-camera eyes, waiting to jump on
anyone who happened to stretch their neck, or blink too many times.
We couldn't move. We couldn't talk. We couldn't think. We could only
hold these emotions inside. And then it started to happen. I began to
feel a low, familiar rumbling deep inside my bowels. You see, I always get
terrible gas when I'm nervous. And I was nervous plus over this test.
Inside me was a gas bubble the size of a beach ball, desperately trying to
get out. Knocking with a heavy determined fist at my back door. Oh, I
tried to suppress it, but it started to expand—the pressure was unbelievable. It got to the point where I didn't even dare shift my leg in fear that
the corral gate would fly open. And the quiet, God was it quiet! Nothing
to cover the impending sound; nothing that would allow me to let out
some of the pressure. Then, without warning, the bubble pushed forward and exploded from me with an ear splitting thunder-gust! A force
so great it lifted me off my desk chair. That was followed by the sound
of 312 snapping necks as they turned around to look at the source of this
deafening blast. The Test Monitors' eyes dilated in angry disbelief. My
fellow students faces twisted like cheap Halloween masks, as they tried
to contain their laughter. That was the final straw. "Who are you to
judge me?!" I screamed out loud. *(Pause.)* What happened to me that day
quickly became legend. Go ahead and tell all you meet. I am not
ashamed.

SCENE XI

Scott is working on his lap-top computer, Clorissa crosses and sits next to him.

CLORISSA: Hey Scott.

SCOTT: Hi Clorissa.

CLORISSA: Is that your new laptop? Nice piece of hardware! *(Notices.)* Wow, you've even logged onto the internet through your cell phone. I'm so jealous.

SCOTT: Your system isn't that bad.

CLORISSA: It's not mine, it's the family's. Besides, I have to schedule an appointment just to get any time on it...

(They are interrupted by Cynthia; Scott melts when he sees her.)

CYNTHIA: Scottie...there you are. I've been looking all over for you.

CLORISSA: *(Sarcastic.)* Cynthia, aren't you taking a major risk being seen over here in the loser hall?

(Cynthia ignores Clorissa and sits next to Scott on the other side. She turns on the charm.)

CYNTHIA: Is that your new computer?

SCOTT: *(Stumbling.)* Uh...yeah...it's...uh...new.

CYNTHIA: It sure is pretty.

CLORISSA: Pretty? Gimmee a break.

CYNTHIA: *(Charm.)* Scottie, I was wondering if you could come over tonight and help me again with my computer.

SCOTT: What's the problem?

CYNTHIA: *(Excited.)* I got another e-mail from HIM!

SCOTT: Kevin, the college hottie?

CYNTHIA: Yes!

SCOTT: I told you all you have to do is click on the icon...uh, picture of the envelope.

CYNTHIA: I did that, but he sent *(Remembering.)* an "image file" or something like that...he said it was another picture of him. I've just got to see it. If it's anything like the last one he sent...*(Explains.)* I tried to "unload" it, but I couldn't get it to work.

CLORISSA: The word is "download"...you couldn't download the picture.

CYNTHIA: Whatever? *(To Scott.)* Would you be an angel and come over and help me tonight?

SCOTT: Uh...sure...be glad to.

CYNTHIA: Oh, thank you! You're such a good guy. A real bud, you know. *(Getting up.)* See you tonight, Scottie.

(She exits.)

CLORISSA: *(Mocking.)* A real bud, you know.

SCOTT: Don't start, Clorissa.

CLORISSA: I just hate the way she uses you.

SCOTT: It's okay…I want to be used.

CLORISSA: She can't even download a picture. My five-year-old brother can do that without any help.

SCOTT: This way I get to spend some time with her.

CLORISSA: If you like her so much…why don't you ask her out?

SCOTT: I don't have a chance with Cynthia and you know it. This way, at least I get to be around her. A friend is better than nothing at all.

CLORISSA: So you're not going to tell her that you are really "Kevin" the chatroom college hottie?

SCOTT: No way.

CLORISSA: This whole thing seems kinda sick to me.

SCOTT: It's not sick, it's romantic. Kevin is everything I'm not. Older. Experienced. Athletic.

CLORISSA: But it's a lie.

SCOTT: *(Emphatic.)* Not the words. Those are mine.

CLORISSA: You're a regular cyberspace Cyrano.

SCOTT: Exactly.

CLORISSA: What about the pictures you send her?

SCOTT: I get them from my brother. They're pictures of his roommate at the university. Guy's pretty good-looking.

CLORISSA: Well, still seems strange to me. But, whatever makes your hard drive happy. *(Looks at watch.)* Want to go grab some pizza?

SCOTT: Can't, got some work to do.

CLORISSA: Well, the more cholesterol for me. See ya later.

(Clorissa exits. Scott starts typing on the keyboard.)

SCOTT: "Cynthia…What's up, babe? Just got outta football practice. I'm sweatin' like a pig, but I know you like stuff like that. Really kicked some butt in practice today. Now I'm just gonna lay back and drink some brews. Hope you liked the picture…send me one of you. I'll have it blown up and put it over my Pamela Lee poster. She's gettin' too old anyway. Well, I gotta go. Later. Your love servant, Kevin."

(Scott smiles and logs off. He closes his laptop and exits with an extra spring in his step.)

SCENE XII

Several students enter, each reads a paperback book; they sit. Claire and Amber enter from opposite sides of the stage; they run into each other because both have their noses buried in a book. The other Students will be the voices of Claire's and Amber's narrative.

CLAIRE: "Sorry, Amber."

STUDENT #1: Claire says out loud, feeling foolish that she wasn't watching where she was going.

STUDENT #2: Amber smiles, realizing that it's her best friend, Claire.

AMBER: "Hi, Claire. Whatcha reading?"

STUDENT #3: Claire hesitates, does she dare reveal that it is yet another trashy romance novel?

STUDENT #2: She decides to since Amber is also an avid romance novel reader.

CLAIRE: "It's called *The Pirates of Love Cove.*"

STUDENT #3: Amber gasps, she too has read this book.

AMBER: "Have you gotten to the part where Peter rescues Madelynn and…"

STUDENT #1: She stops, not wanting to give away the entire plot.

STUDENT #2: Claire eyes Amber with contempt.

CLAIRE: "No, and you've just ruined it for me."

AMBER: "Sorry, I thought you would be further along."

STUDENT #3: She says with a smirk, knowing that she reads twice as fast as Claire.

STUDENT #2: Hiding her anger, Claire fights to control herself…

STUDENT #1: Amber thinks about going for blood, but knows that Claire has a much larger collection of books than she.

AMBER: "Sorry, I didn't mean anything by that."

STUDENT #3: She's pretending, Claire thinks to herself. She's after my books.

AMBER: "Isn't it lame that we can't do book reports on these for Mrs. Lindstrom's class?"

CLAIRE: "Yes."

STUDENT #1,#2, #3: Claire says in total agreement.

AMBER: "Oh well. Listen…"

STUDENT #1: Amber realizes time is growing short.

AMBER: "Are you finished reading *Lust in My Life?*"

STUDENT #3: Knowing Amber wants to borrow it, Claire contemplates whether she will give up the prized prose.

CLAIRE: "Yes, as a matter of fact I have."

STUDENT #1: Claire purses her lips coyly, knowing the butt kissing will come any moment…

AMBER: "Since you're such a good friend…and generous person…"

STUDENT #2: Amber lies through her teeth…

AMBER: "Could I borrow it?"

STUDENT #1: Claire toys with her for a moment and then makes a grand nod of the head as her lips break into a condescending smile…

CLAIRE: "Sure…come over tonight and it's yours."

STUDENT #3: Relieved that she didn't have to grovel more, Amber says…

AMBER: "Thanks, Claire. See ya later then?"

CLAIRE: "Yes, later."

STUDENT #2: Realizing the time, Claire heads to another dreary Biology class.

(Claire exits, followed by Student #2.)

STUDENT #1: Amber thinks for a moment and then decides that hiding out in the library and reading *The Love Cop* will be much more fun than going to class.

STUDENT #3: And so, with a mischievous grin…she heads for the door.

(Amber opens her book and begins to read as she exits, followed by Student #1 and #3, who do the same.)

SCENE XIII

Maggie, a shy girl, sits holding a boom box tape player that plays classical music. She sits and as the music fades she turns the player off. Herm, a nerdy boy, enters holding a boom box tape player as well. His is playing some upbeat dance music and he awkwardly tries to move to the beat. He crosses and sits near Maggie. They smile at each other, both are a bit shy but interested. Herm's music fades out and then the tape says….

HERM'S TAPED VOICE: The lunch room was really crowded today, wasn't it?
(*All of the lines in this scene will be pre-taped using the actor's voices. Each actor will have only their lines on their tape and will play the tape one line at a time. They simulate dialog by pushing the pause button while the other is

speaking and then releasing it for their line. The actors should physically react to the lines their tape is speaking, but not mouth the words.)

MAGGIE'S TAPED VOICE: Yes, that's why I came out here to the court-yard.

HERM'S TAPED VOICE: Looks like it might rain.

MAGGIE'S TAPED VOICE: The weatherman said it might.

HERM'S TAPED VOICE: Aren't you in my English class?

MAGGIE's TAPED VOICE: Yes, I sit three rows back from you.

HERM'S TAPED VOICE: Your name is… Maggie.

MAGGIE'S TAPED VOICE: And yours is Herm.

HERM'S TAPED VOICE: I liked the report you did on Walt Whitman.

MAGGIE'S TAPED VOICE: You did? Well, I liked your report on the song lyrics of Marilyn Manson, too.

HERM'S TAPED VOICE: I thought it was good, but Mr. Slater only gave me a C because he doesn't consider that kind of music literary.

MAGGIE'S TAPED VOICE: Well it is…kinda.

(Herm moves closer to Maggie.)

HERM'S TAPED VOICE: Are you going to the game this Friday?

MAGGIE'S TAPED VOICE: I have to stay home and baby-sit my little brother. Are you?

HERM'S TAPED VOICE: I have to, I'm the team manager.

MAGGIE'S TAPED VOICE: Wow, that's a real honor.

HERM'S TAPED VOICE: Most people don't think so.

MAGGIE'S TAPED VOICE: Well I do.

(Herm looks at watch.)

HERM'S TAPED VOICE: Lunch time is almost over. I'd better go.

(He gets up and starts to leave.)

MAGGIE'S TAPED VOICE: It was nice talking with you.

HERM'S TAPED VOICE: You too…uh…I was wondering…well…uh maybe we could…

MAGGIE'S TAPED VOICE: *(Finishing for him.)*…meet tomorrow out here and talk again?

HERM'S TAPED VOICE: You took the words right outta my…uh…whatever. I'd like that, Maggie.

MAGGIE'S TAPED VOICE: Then I'll see you tomorrow, Herm.

(Herm smiles at her and then exits. Maggie smiles and classical music starts to play again on her tape player.)

SCENE XIV

Mirelle enters holding a large envelope. She starts to open it and then seals it back closed.

MIRELLE: Thank God this is the last year I'm going to have to go through this. Some people just don't photograph well. I don't photograph well. But every year my Mom insists that I get these stupid class pictures taken. She just doesn't understand. *(Starts to open envelope; quickly closes it.)* I can't look. They're gonna be awful. Just like every year. It wasn't so bad when I was in grade school. I mean, all kids are cute…in a kid kind of way. But lately, yikes! My Freshman year I had "red-eye," you know, like cats have at night. Sophomore pictures would have been okay if the photographer hadn't caught me in "mid-blink"…I looked like I was stoned or something. Last year, I had a bad hair day. You think I'm making too much out of this? Well keep in mind that these pictures don't just sit in Aunt Bessie's drawer. They go right into the yearbook… enshrined forever like a museum of frightening photos. Someone told me they use them on name-badges at class reunions…for the rest of our lives! *(Pause.)* Alright, there's only one way to do this. Like a pond of water. Dive right in. *(Pulls the proof sheet out and looks at photos; pause.)* Hey… these aren't bad. Not bad at all. I mean, I'm no "cover girl" but these are alright. Finally. Thank you, Jesus! I can live with these. *(Relieved laugh.)* I can live with these!

SCENE XV
JACK HELLER REVISITED

Jack sits looking at a picture in a large book. He turns the book to look at it with a different perspective. Joni approaches him.

JONI: What's up Mr. Three-home-runs-in-one-game-all-conference star?
JACK: A little homework.
JONI: You put this school on the baseball map…you shouldn't have to bother with anything as lame as homework.
JACK: I wish.
JONI: Don't tell me…Mr. Kelsey is making you study weird paintings?

JACK: Somethin' like that.

JONI: I had him last semester.

JACK: I know.

JONI: You have to write a paper on one of those arty paintings.

JACK: Right…

JONI: *(Imitating Kelsey.)* "What do I see in this picture?"

JACK: You really got him down.

JONI: You know I always did pretty good in Kelsey's class, 'specially with stuff like this. Let me look at it…

(Joni takes the book from him, studies the picture.)

JONI: Hmmm, well, I see a clown…eating cotton candy. And this line here is like a tightrope. Look there *(Points.)* that could be an elephant. So write about that. Tell him you think it looks like a circus.

JACK: *(Looks at picture.)* A circus?

JONI: Pretty good, huh?

JACK: Yeah, I didn't see that in there.

JONI: I have a real eye for stuff like this. Guys just don't have much imagination when it comes to art. Geez, if I left it up to you you'd probably just see cars, hot babes, and baseballs.

JACK: You're probably right.

JONI: Trust me, the circus thing is the way to go with this one. *(Looks at watch.)* Gotta run. See you later.

JACK: Thanks Joni…see ya.

(Joni exits. Jack opens the book back up to the picture.)

JACK: "What do I see in this picture?" *(Studies the picture; he stands and is obviously inspired.)* I see an intergalactic clipper ship sailing across the windswept seas of uncharted space. *(Building.)* The massive sail billows with a strong gust from the constellation Orion. *(Stands on cube; louder, more dramatic.)* The Captain stands at the bow. His only map is the parchment woven from the fiber of his soul. He embraces the impending journey, the pilgrimage. Ready to sail into the electrifying abyss of discovery!

(Another Student, enters and spots Jack, who becomes self-conscious. Jack makes a quick exit.)

SCENE XVI

Martha watches other happy students as they make their way to class. She addresses the audience.

MARTHA: I spend a lot of time just hangin' in the halls, checkin' out some of the kids in this school. I start thinkin' about what it would be like to be them, to live their lives. And I wonder what it must be like to live in a house that has plenty of room. In a neighborhood where helicopters don't fly overhead all night long. I wonder what it would be like to have both a Mom and a Dad. To not worry about my little sister gettin' hit with a stray bullet because somebody's fightin' over a street they don't even own. To have my own bedroom where I have my own things that no one will mess with. To not have to watch my brother racing to the grave with a never-ending need for twenty dollar pieces of rock. And I wonder what it's like to go places—like the beach, another state, another country. To go somewhere…anywhere. To not worry about the electricity bein' turned off, or the car bein' repo'ed. I wonder what it's like to have dreams instead of nightmares and to know that those dreams someday may actually come true. To look through brochures of colleges and universities and know that I have a choice. To see myself living long enough to become an adult. *(She watches several more students as they walk past her.)* And as I watch the lucky ones, I wonder most of all, what it would be like to have hope. To have just a little bit of hope. *(Martha exits.)*

SCENE XVII

Kyle sits very still on a cube.

KYLE: What I really want to know is if anybody has a videotape of the game. Anybody? You see, everything was so confusing that I don't remember much about it. All I really remember is the pass…Diggs always throws too far, so I had to kick in the afterburners to reach the ball. I know I beat the man that was coverin' me, 'cause I saw his red shirt behind me. The ball was just out of my reach so I had to leap like a bullfrog to grab it. I remember hittin' the ground and a bunch of people on top of me. And then darkness. When I came to I heard a guy say, "Some sort of fluke." I thought he was talkin' about my great catch, but then I hear 'em talkin' about my head and neck. Then bright lights. More people. But we weren't on the football field anymore. And then...(Thinks.) Well, the rest is all kinda fuzzy. Not quite sure. (Pause.) The doctors say I'll never walk again. That this chair will be part of me for life. But I know I'm gonna get out of this thing. No matter what, I am gonna walk again. (Pause.) I hope somebody has a tape. 'Cause I really want to see myself making that game winning catch. Running like the wind and making that catch!

SCENE XVIII

Felicia enters and spots Nate.

FELECIA: Where were you last night?

NATE: Uh...like I told you. I was fishing.

FELECIA: (Severe.) I know, Nate. Karla told me...she saw you at the restaurant. With some lady...a blonde. You obviously like older women.

NATE: It's not what you think. I wasn't on a date...That woman is my... mother.

FELECIA: Gimmee a break. I know your mother, she has black hair and happens to be in Europe on vacation. I'm outta here... (Felecia starts off.)

NATE: I was adopted. (Felecia stops.)

FELECIA: You never told me you were adopted.

NATE: I never told anybody.

FELECIA: And the blonde is your real Mother?

NATE: Yes...and last night was the first time I've ever seen her. She called me a few days ago...really caught me by surprise. Wanted to meet me.

FELECIA: I thought if you give up a baby...they won't tell you where it goes.

NATE: She has a lot of money. Married some rich guy. When you have money you can find out just about anything you want.

FELECIA: So you agreed to meet her?

NATE: I was curious. On the way over I thought about the questions I had for her: Why did you do it? Why couldn't you have found a way to keep me? I was pretty angry when I got to the restaurant. I was just gonna tell her off and then go.

FELECIA: So why didn't you?

NATE: When she introduced herself, she kinda fell apart. Started crying and hugging me. So I calmed her down and suggested we eat dinner. I figured it would be easier to talk to her if there was people around. *(Pause.)* She told me she was only seventeen when she had me. That she didn't even know who the father was 'cause she slept with several guys. Then she apologized for five minutes. Said she was gonna keep me, but her parents woulda kicked her out of the house if she did. She gave me up so I would at least have a good home.

FELECIA: Which you do.

NATE: Yes I do...and I told her that. Anyway, after she married the rich guy a few years ago she started lookin' for me. It didn't take long. She's known about me for awhile, but it took her some time to get up the courage to call me.

FELECIA: Sounds like she had a pretty rough life.

NATE: I know, even though that doesn't make up for what she did. Then, the more I talked to her...she became a person to me, instead of some stranger. Not a mom or anything, but not a stranger either. It's weird, but I started feeling sorry for her.

FELECIA: So then what happened?

NATE: We finished dinner and she gave me her number. Told me that she wouldn't call me. That she would stay away unless I wanted to talk to her. It's all my choice.

FELECIA: Are you going to tell your parents...I mean the ones you live with?

NATE: Not right now. I don't want them to worry about me. They'd probably think I don't love them as much now. But the truth is...I think I love them even more.

FELECIA: Nate, I'm sorry I was mad at you. Do you want to be alone for awhile?

NATE: Not really.

FELECIA: Why don't we go over to my place? Kelly's got band practice so we'd have the pool all to ourselves.

NATE: Alright.

(They start to head out.)

FELECIA: There is one major downside to all of this.

NATE: What's that?

FELECIA: *(Gentle.)* Mother's Day is sure gonna be expensive for you. *(Quickly.)* Sorry, bad joke.

NATE: *(Smiles.)* Don't be sorry. Maybe that's the kind of stuff I need to hear right now.

(Nate puts his arm around Felecia and they exit.)

SCENE XIX

Pete and Paul Johnson enter; they wear matching glasses and hats to give the illusion that they are twin brothers.

PETE & PAUL: We're the Johnsons.

PETE: He's Paul.

PAUL: And he's Pete.

PETE & PAUL: We're twin brothers.

PETE: Have been all our lives.

(They laugh at their favorite joke.)

PAUL: We're also best friends.

PETE: We do everything together.

PAUL: People say that twins have some kind of weird psychic connection.

PETE: They're right.

PAUL: I feel his pain sometimes.

PETE: And I feel his.

PAUL: I read an article that said it has something to do with being in the womb together.

PETE: I read it, too.

PAUL: It doesn't bother us that some of the other students tease us about looking alike.

PETE: They're just jealous because they don't have a close friend who's also their brother, like Paul.

PAUL: Or like Pete.

PETE: They think we still dress alike because our Mom makes us.

PAUL: Not true, we still dress alike so we can fool our teachers.

PETE: You see, Paul is really good at Math.

PAUL: And Pete is really good at Science.

PETE & PAUL: We take tests for each other!

(They laugh at their second favorite joke.)

PETE: He's Pete.

PAUL: And he's Paul.

PETE & PAUL: *(To audience.)* Gotcha…
PAUL: *(Pointing.)* He's Pete!
PETE: *(Pointing.)* And he's Paul!
PAUL & PETE: We're twin brothers.
(They exit with the same walk.)

SCENE XX

Stacy enters, looking at a yearbook for a moment and then notices the audience.

STACY: The new yearbook just came out. For all the problems this school has, they at least understand the importance of letting us get our yearbooks signed. In the old days we had to do it between classes, or before and after school. That's just not enough time to trade books and do all that signing. Now they give us a whole hour during the day.
(She looks at her book and a light comes up on another Student who is speaking what she reads—or they can just enter, say their piece, and then exit.)
STUDENT #1: Stacy, it's been a great year. If you wouldn't have been in Math class with me, I would have crawled the walls. Here's to next year when we're Seniors! Ellen.
STACY: You see, the words our friends write in these books are very important. Not so much for now, but for later when we're older and look back.
(Another Student is lit.)
STUDENT #2: Stace, Well one more year and we're out of this brain factory. See you at the mall this summer. Bobby.
STACY: For some people these years may be the best of their entire lives, and the friends we make here will be friends forever.
STUDENT #3: Williams, you loser. I'm using my red ink pen on your book because I want to save the good pen for cool people. Just kidding, Stewart.
STACY: And some you hope you never see again. But no matter what they write, it'll be a memory that will bring a future smile.
STUDENT #4: Lacey-Stacy, you're the best friend ever, and just knowing you has made my life better. Don't ever forget me, because I will never forget you. Always, Debbie.
STACY: They may seem like simple words, but years from now they will be

an important connection to the past. They will be our souvenirs, waiting for us on a page…whenever we need to remember.
(She turns the page, continues to read as she exits.)

SCENE XXI

Linda enters and starts to cross stage left, she sees Darren enter from the other side and turns around to avoid him.

DARREN: Linda, wait up…
(Darren crosses quickly to Linda; she stops.)
DARREN: I've been looking all over for you. Where have you been?
LINDA: I was out this morning.
DARREN: That's a relief, I thought you were avoiding me or somethin'.
LINDA: Avoiding you is what I should have done last night.
DARREN: Oh come on, are you still mad at me about that?
LINDA: *(Dismayed.)* "That"?
DARREN: *(Changing the subject.)* I wanted to give you a present. I know your birthday is a month away, but I thought that everyone would give you something then…I'd be different and give you something now.
(He hands her a small wrapped gift; Linda doesn't accept it.)
DARREN: Come on. It's that sports watch you wanted. You know, the one you can wear even when you scuba dive. *(Off her stare.)* What?
LINDA: You really think you can right this wrong with a stupid watch?
DARREN: Right this wrong? Oh, come on, Linda…*(Pause.)* Alright, I admit I was a little outta line last night.
LINDA: You were way out of line last night, Darren. You crossed over it…all the way over.
DARREN: You know I had too much to drink. I wasn't really in control. *(Defensive.)* Besides, like they say…"It takes two."
LINDA: Not last night it didn't. It was all just you.
DARREN: Look, I'm sorry. What do you want me say?
LINDA: I don't want you to say anything…as a matter of fact I don't want to ever talk to you again.
DARREN: You're makin' too much outta this, Linda.
LINDA: I don't think so.

DARREN: Don't be stupid here...you've got a pretty good thing goin' with me. I could have my choice of girls...and I chose you. So don't ruin it.

LINDA: I already "ruined it," Darren. About an hour ago.

DARREN: What are you talking about? *(Concerned.)* Where were you this morning?

LINDA: At the Police Station...filing a report. Filing a report against you.

DARREN: What? A report against me? This is insane. No one's gonna believe you.

LINDA: They did.

DARREN: You little... *(Pause.)* This is incredible. And after all I've done for you.

LINDA: After all you've done to me.

DARREN: Oh, man...You went to the police? Just because we had a little fun?

LINDA: It wasn't fun.

DARREN: You totally misread where I was comin' from. I just wanted to show you that I liked you. That you were special.

LINDA: You're pathetic.

DARREN: This isn't happening. Why, Linda? Why are you doing this to me when I didn't do anything wrong?

LINDA: That's exactly why I'm doing it, Darren. Because you don't think you did anything wrong.

VOICE ON THE INTERCOM: "Darren Post, please report to the Front Office. Darren Post."

(It starts to sink into Darren's head. Linda takes a deep breath, composes herself, and then exits.)

SCENE XXII

Brenda and Gail face the audience as they put on makeup, looking into a fake mirror.

BRENDA: I think you need more rouge.

GAIL: I'm fine.

BRENDA: You wanna skip outta Psych class and go over to the mall?

GAIL: Last time we did that we got caught.

BRENDA: That's because we took Denise with us...she's like a jinx or something.

GAIL: She used to be your best friend.

BRENDA: Well that ended when I found out she was hitting on my boyfriend.

GAIL: That'll do it.

BRENDA: She didn't even deny it. Well, I told her our friendship was over. Real friends don't do that to you.

GAIL: I never would.

BRENDA: That's exactly what I said to Denise. "Gail would never do that to me." And do you know what she said? She said, "Of course not, because Gail is funny."

GAIL: I'm funny?

BRENDA: Not ha-ha, stand-up type funny...more like queer-type funny. You know, "lesbo-land."

GAIL: She said that, huh?

BRENDA: Imagine that. She thinks you're gay.

GAIL: That's because I am.

BRENDA: *(Laughs.)* Yeah right.
    (Brenda realizes Gail isn't laughing.)

BRENDA: You're kidding, of course.

GAIL: No, I'm not.

BRENDA: You mean you're not gay...

GAIL: I mean I'm not kidding.

BRENDA: That's ridiculous. I would know...I'm your best friend.

GAIL: Yes, you are.

BRENDA: So if you were a...you know...I would certainly be the first one you would tell.

GAIL: I've thought about telling you many, many times. I even wrote down how I was going to say it. Long speeches. Full of explanations and revelations. But I always choked when it came time to fill you in. But now, it just kinda came out. It was so easy. Just a few words and there it is. I'm out.
    (Brenda is stunned.)

BRENDA: I can't believe it. We've known each other since we were three. When did this happen?

GAIL: Probably a long time ago. I'm not sure.

BRENDA: But you're too young to be a lesbian.

GAIL: What?

BRENDA: Well, I mean it's...I'm confused.

GAIL: I went through some of that myself.

BRENDA: Do your parents know?

GAIL: Not yet. I think my dad would understand, but my mom would freak. I don't want to hurt her, but I guess someday she'll have to be told.

BRENDA: This is terrible.

GAIL: What's so terrible? You've known me for a long time. It never affected us before.

BRENDA: I never knew about your condition before.

GAIL: It's not a condition...it's a lifestyle. Besides, your uncle is gay and you don't have a problem with that.

BRENDA: Because I only see him about once a year.

GAIL: But he's your favorite uncle.

BRENDA: He's my favorite uncle because he sends me fifty bucks on my birthday.

GAIL: So how much do I have to pay you to accept me?

(Brenda doesn't react to that, she's too busy trying to deal with what Gail has revealed.)

BRENDA: God, Gail...like ruin my day in a major way.

GAIL: I'm sorry. I think it's time you knew.

BRENDA: But this changes everything.

GAIL: How?

BRENDA: Well, for starters, what if you get the hots for me? That totally freaks me out. I don't feel safe anymore.

GAIL: Let me explain something to you, Brenda. I know that you are straight and I respect that. I've never done anything in the past and don't plan to in the future. I'm just your friend, nothing more. *(Pause.)* Besides, I'm not interested in you...you're just not my type.

BRENDA: I don't know about this. Like, I'm gonna need some time to sort this all out.

(Gail starts to leave.)

GAIL: Take all the time you want, Brenda. But don't expect me to sit around and wait for you. I've got my life to live.

(Gail exits. Brenda thinks for a moment, fighting through the confusion. Suddenly, she thinks of something even more confusing.)

BRENDA: Wait a minute... "I'm not your type?" What did she mean by that? *(Touches her face.)* Gail...Gail?

(Brenda exits.)

SCENE XXIII

Scooter paces back and forth; he starts to address someone who is not there. He is practicing.

SCOOTER: Janine, I was wondering if you...*(New approach.)* Janine, the dance is this weekend and I thought if you weren't doing anything... *(Again.)* Janine we've been friends for a long time and I think it's time we get serious about each other...Janine... *(Janine enters.)* Janine!

JANINE: Who you talking to?

SCOOTER: Nobody, just...uh...myself.

JANINE: Well, now that I'm here you can talk to me.

SCOOTER: Right, as a matter of fact...

JANINE: Because I really need someone to talk to right now. I am stressing out.

SCOOTER: What's wrong?

JANINE: I have to make a big decision and I don't know what to do. You know there's this dance next Saturday.

SCOOTER: *(Ironic.)* I think I heard something about it.

JANINE: Today in third period I get a note from Randy Williams.

SCOOTER: He can write actual words?

JANINE: I'm serious. He asked me to go to the dance with him, whether they win the game or not.

SCOOTER: *(Hides his reaction.)* Sounds pretty serious.

JANINE: Tell me about it. So, anyway, as I'm writing him back, I get another note from Alan Michaels, asking me to go to the dance with him. So I wrote them both back and told them I would let them know by the end of the day.

SCOOTER: You got two more hours.

JANINE: And I still haven't decided. That's why I need your help.

SCOOTER: You want me to go out with one of them?

JANINE: Will you stop? *(Serious.)* Scooter, you are the only person I can talk to about this. Not only are you my best friend, you're also a guy.

SCOOTER: *(Aside.)* Glad you noticed.

JANINE: I trust your advice. You're like a brother to me.

(Scooter takes a few steps away, hiding his hurt reaction.)

SCOOTER: Well, let's look at this logically. You've dated Randy before and didn't have a very good time because he's so into himself. However, he's the star quarterback and that would increase your stock in every social circle around here.

JANINE: You know every shallow thing about me.

SCOOTER: *(Firm.)* There's nothing shallow about you and I hate it when you put yourself down.

JANINE: I'm sorry.

SCOOTER: On the other hand, although Alan is a pretty good-looking guy, he's got those allergies. I've never seen anybody blow his nose as much as that guy…he's a one-man-mucus-machine. My advice is to go with Randy…and take a mirror so he can admire himself if he gets bored with you.

JANINE: You really think I should go with Randy?

SCOOTER: In all seriousness, he's the best choice.

JANINE: That's what I hoped you would say.

(She hugs Scooter.)

JANINE: I don't know what I'd do without you.

SCOOTER: You better go find him, before he asks someone else.

JANINE: You're right.

(She starts to leave.)

JANINE: I'll call you later and let you know how it went.

SCOOTER: Great.

JANINE: You are the best.

(She exits, leaving Scooter to his own thoughts.)

SCENE XXIV

A nerdy Student enters. He wears a black leather jacket, but his posture and demeanor don't fit the jacket.

SPIKE: Most kids would think that moving a thousand miles to a new school their sophomore year would be a real bust. I did too, at first. But then I started thinking about my life up until that point. How I had turned out the way my parents wanted me, instead of how I wanted me. And then it hit me like a thunderbolt. This move gives me a second chance. To be someone else. To change all the stuff I hated about my life. You see, here, no one would know that I was a button-down-dressing, middle-class-living, honor roll-achieving, Boy Scout-belonging, parent-proud-acting, dork named Lyle Kidman. Instead, they would know me only as *(Puts on a pair of severe sunglasses; adapts a cool pose.)* Spike. The bad boy from Boston. The dark stranger of mystery.

(Two girls enter and see him; they think he's hot.)

GIRL #1: Hi Spike...

GIRL #2: Love your leather.

SPIKE: *(Very cool.)* Whass up, honeys?

(The girls exit.)

SPIKE: *(Tips his shades down to audience.)* It's gonna be a great year!

(He puts his glasses back up and struts offstage.)

SCENE XXV

LEAZA: I was the one who found her. They say it's a miracle that I came home when I did. From the start I knew something wasn't right. Her car was parked kinda funny in the driveway. It was only 3:30 and she was supposed to be at work. Also, the front door was unlocked...that seemed pretty weird too. *(Pause.)* I heard the water running and normally I wouldn't have thought much of that, but it seemed so loud 'cause there was no TV on, no loud music, none of the things Haley usually did when she came home. The psychiatrist, Dr. Linda, told me that the fact the bathroom door was unlocked meant she wanted to be found. I'm not so sure about that. I opened the door and saw her there in the shower... sitting against the shower wall. She was still conscious but had lost a lot of blood. There was a note taped to the mirror...right above the razor blade. Didn't really say why, just that she was sorry and she loved all of us. *(Pause.)* Dad was really torn up about this, I think Mom was mostly embarrassed. She wanted us to keep it a family secret, but Dr. Linda set her straight about that. That something like this needs to be brought out and looked at from all angles. They say it will take Haley a long time to get over this and we all have to keep an eye on her, but not be too over-protective. It's a fine line, they say. She may do it again, or maybe not. We all go to meetings a couple times a week. I don't think I can ever talk to Haley the way I used to. *(Pause.)* I was the one that found her.

SCENE XXVI

Carmen enters holding a file folder in her hands.

CARMEN: *(To audience.)* Mr. Carlyle accidently dropped a copy of our Science final on the floor. He didn't see it fall, but I did. After he left the room I picked it up. I haven't looked at it yet, but I bet there are a lot of kids who would love to have a copy of this. I know I would. But I also know that it would be wrong.
(Carolyn and Antoinette enter and flank her on either side. They are the opposing voices of her confused conscience and speak to her.)
CAROLYN: If it was wrong then why did fate put that test in your hands? It's a karma thing. You've worked hard all semester yet you'll be lucky to get a C in his class. This is payback, that's all. For all your hard work.
ANTOINETTE: Hard work is its own reward. Looking at that test ahead of time isn't right and you know it. You may not have a high grade in the class, but you do have your integrity.
CAROLYN: Integrity doesn't buy you that trip to Palm Springs your parents promised if you make the Honor Roll. You want to spend another year down at the tanning salon, or gettin' the real deal?
ANTOINETTE: There's still a chance you can do well on that test without looking at it. Study hard, then when you ace it you'll feel a lot better than if you cheated.
CAROLYN: It's not cheating, it's just being prepared. Information is power. Use it! Or suffer the consequences. And if you want some extra spending money for your trip, you could make a fortune selling copies of that thing.
ANTOINETTE: Selling copies? It's bad enough if you look at that test, but if you sell it to others then you could go to jail!
CAROLYN: *(To Antoinette.)* You can't go to jail for selling a science test. Are you outta your mind?
ANTOINETTE: *(To Carolyn.)* No, I'm outta her mind. Just like you are. And I'm prepared to do anything I can to prevent her from making a wrong turn.
CAROLYN: Wrong turn, this ain't no driving class, it's science class. Her worst subject.
ANTOINETTE: Only because you talked her into going skating instead of studying for her midterm.

CAROLYN: Well, she only skated for an hour before you made her feel guilty and she came back home…

(Carmen takes the test out of her folder.)

ANTOINETTE: Oh no, she's taking out the test.

CAROLYN: You go girl!

ANTOINETTE: Don't do it Carmen. It'll be the biggest mistake of your life.

CAROLYN: And the best report card of your life.

(Carmen closes her eyes and turns the test on it's side, begins to rip it into pieces.)

ANTOINETTE: All right, Carmen!

CAROLYN: Oh no…nooooooo!

(Carmen tosses the pieces into a nearby trash can and then starts to exit. Antoinette and Carolyn follow her off, arguing all the way.)

ANTOINETTE: That's my girl.

CAROLYN: Why do you always get to have your way?

ANTOINETTE: I don't always get my way. Like yesterday when she skipped out of Government class to go get ice cream.

CAROLYN: You thought that was wrong?

(They are gone.)

SCENE XXVII

Jim and Bruno sit and watch as several students walk by; Jim makes comments as they pass.

JIM: Hey, Cathy…thanks a lot for throwin' the curve off on the Chemistry test. (Pause.) Roberto…strong look, my man. (Pause.) Toni…call me later. (Ronny, a disheveled and nervous boy, enters pushing a rolling cart with a video player and monitor.)

JIM: (To Bruno.) Can you believe this?

BRUNO: Don't start, Jim. Jesus, leave the guy alone for once, will ya? (Ronny tries to walk by them quickly, Jim stops him with.)

JIM: Hold up there, Ron-Job. What do you think you're doin'? (He crosses to Ronny.)

RONNY: Oh, hi Jim. I'm takin' this to Mr. Remsen.

JIM: Through the East Hall? Ronny, today is the seventh. That's an odd-numbered day. And you're only allowed to walk in the East Hall on even-numbered days.

RONNY: I am?

JIM: That's right. We all had a meeting and decided that. Right Bruno?

BRUNO: No.

RONNY: I didn't know about no meeting.

JIM: That's 'cause you were probably at one of your retard classes over at your other special school.

BRUNO: Jim…

(Ronny starts to exit, but Jim blocks his way.)

JIM: Where do you think you're goin'?

RONNY: I got to take this to Mr. Remsen.

JIM: Wow, that sounds real important, Ron-Job. But that will have to wait.

RONNY: He's showin' the movie first thing, so I gotta go right now.

BRUNO: Let him go.

JIM: I will, Bruno, just as soon as he pays the fine for walking in the East Hall on the wrong day.

RONNY: But Mr. Remsen is waitin' for me, Jim.

JIM: He's gonna have to wait a little longer. You broke the rules, you gotta pay.

(Ronny pulls some change from his pocket.)

JIM: That's not enough, Ron-Job. But I'll tell you what, I'll just assign you a penalty instead of a fine.

BRUNO: Jim we're gonna be late for class. Let's go.

JIM: *(Ignores Bruno.)* Let's see. The penalty for walking in a restricted area and gettin' in my way is…*(Thinks.)* to bark like a dog.

RONNY: I gotta go. Mr. Remsen gets real mad when I'm late.

JIM: I don't blame him. But you got business right here first. Do your penalty and then you can go.

BRUNO: That's enough…

JIM: Stay out of it, Bruno. *(To Ronny.)* Come on start barkin', retard.

RONNY: I'm not a retard!

JIM: You're right…it's your Dad that's retarded. You're just an idiot.

RONNY: Don't talk about my Dad.

JIM: I'll talk about anything I want. This is my hall and you're trespassing.

RONNY: Don't talk about my Dad.

BRUNO: Stop it, Jim. Ronny, just go ahead to class. He's just kidding.

(Jim gets right in Ronny's face.)

JIM: No I'm not, Ron-Job. I'm serious about this. You better bark like I told you or you're never gonna make it to Remsens. Now, do it! *(Ronny starts to bark softly.)* I can't hear you! *(Ronny barks louder.)* Dogs don't stand on two legs. Get on all fours!

(Ronny stops; looks around at several students who have gathered.)

JIM: I said on all fours!

(Jim grabs Ronny and wrestles him to the ground. Bruno cuts in and pulls Jim off Ronny. He tosses Jim to the side like a rag doll and then crosses to Ronny; helps him up.)

BRUNO: You alright, Ronny?

RONNY: Yeah…can I go to Mr. Remsen's room now?

BRUNO: Go ahead. *(Ronny hesitates.)* It's okay, he's not going to do anything to you. I'll make sure of that.

(Someone rolls the cart to Ronny and he makes a quick exit.)

JIM: *(To Bruno.)* What the hell is wrong with you?

BRUNO: What's wrong with you? You've been terrorizing Ronny ever since we were kids.

JIM: Like I'm the only one.

BRUNO: No, but you're the most vicious. Do you get some kinda high from terrorizing him? Why, because he's weaker? Slower? Are you really that insecure, Jim. You're pathetic, man.

JIM: It's just a joke. He's just a joke.

BRUNO: Well maybe it's not so funny, anymore. And maybe you aren't either.

(The others look at Jim for a moment. They exit, along with Bruno. Leaving Jim alone on stage.)

JIM: I don't believe this.

(Jim looks around and becomes self-conscious; exits.)

SCENE XXVIII

Amy, Jasmine, Zeena, and Eric enter excitedly. They are wearing graduation caps and gowns.

AMY: We call ourselves the "Four-Pack." I'm Amy.

JASMINE: Jasmine…

ERIC: Eric…

ZEENA: Zeena.

JASMINE: We've been good friends for a long time.

ERIC: The four of us go everywhere together, do everything together. 'Specially during the past four years.

AMY: That's why we got the nickname the Four-Pack.

ZEENA: Four years, four friends…

JASMINE: *(Beach accent.)* For sure…

> *(They all laugh; Jasmine, Eric, and Amy pose for a picture. Zeena, with an instamatic camera in hand, turns and talks to the audience.)*

ZEENA: My older sister Zelda hated high school. She warned me how bad it would be so by the time I got here I was scared scatless. But I had a great time. Maybe it didn't seem so bad to me 'cause I had more friends than she did. I think what I'll miss the most about the Four-Pack is how we always watched out for one another. Like those little desert meerkats that live in packs. Zelda never had close friends like these. Now she has two kids, a dog, a parakeet, and a husband who watches every sporting event broadcast on cable. Even water polo. Every time I talk to Zelda she has that glazed look in her eye. I hope I never get that way. I don't think I will.

> *(Zeena takes a picture of the other three and passes the camera to Amy, who talks to the audience.)*

AMY: I always thought our high school years would make a great music video. I'd use a lot of water. Pools. Beach settings. Fish tanks. I think at some point during the video the four of us would be playing instruments that had to do with our personalities. I'd be on drums. Loud drums. And then when all my college friends asked what my high school life was like I could just sit them down and pop in the video. Not that they would really understand, but it would at least be entertaining.

> *(Amy takes a picture of the other three and then hands the camera to Eric, who turns to the audience.)*

ERIC: Why does everyone feel that I'm safe. Like yesterday, I was at the pharmacy and this elderly woman comes up to me and asks me to help her find a good skin creme. I ask you: Do I look like a skin creme authority? It happens to me all the time. Total strangers just come up to me and start talkin' like they know me. Zeena says it's my "boy next door" look. People trust me. I tried to grow a beard this year to make myself look a little edgy, but it just made me look wiser. Wise men just aren't dangerous. Well, at least the Pack knows that I'm more than just the guy next door. That I have a dangerous side. Jasmine said it best. "Eric, I wouldn't trust you if you didn't get some strange ideas once and awhile…people who don't are the most dangerous of all."

> *(He takes a picture of the three and then hands the camera to Jasmine, who talks to the audience.)*

JASMINE: I think a person should have a school locker even at home. Yeah,

I have my own bedroom, but it doesn't have a lock on the door 'cause my Mom says she needs to get in to clean and get my laundry and stuff. I pretend to buy that story, but I know she's snooping. So I keep my secrets at school in my locker. Amy knows the combination, but I never worry about her. She's part of the Pack and we respect each other's property. Maybe that's why I like them a lot more than my family. I think that's the case with most kids. By the time you reach high school you've had enough of your family. You start to put your trust and your hope for the future on others your own age.

(She takes a picture of the other three.)

JASMINE: We call ourselves the Four-Pack. I'm Jasmine.

AMY: Amy...

ERIC: Eric...

ZEENA: Zeena.

JASMINE: Four years, four friends...

AMY: Forever.

CLOSE

A school bell is heard and the rest of the Cast, in regular school clothes, enters and joins the "Four-Pack". They ad-lib about it being the end of the school year. The actor who played Nick in the first scene takes the camera from Jasmine; he crosses downstage center and talks to the audience.

NICK: In high school the real learning takes place outside the classroom— In the halls, before and after school, hanging out in the parking lot and all the other places where we can just be ourselves. That's where we learn about life, love, and how to get along with each other. The things we do outside the classroom will form the foundation on which we build the rest of our lives.

(Nick crosses to an audience member and hands him or her the instamatic camera, indicating that he wants him or her to take a picture. Nick then crosses to the rest of the Group and they quickly form a tableau to pose. And as the picture is taken, the stage lights fade out, leaving them frozen in the tableau.)

END OF PLAY

WHEN THEY SPEAK OF RITA

by Daisy Foote

From the A.C.T. production of *When They Speak of Rita,* by Daisy Foote.
(from left) Caitlin Talbot, Joseph Parks, Diane Curley, and Justin Okin.
Photo by Bob Adler.

ORIGINAL PRODUCTION

When They Speak of Rita was commissioned for and first produced by the Young Conservatory New Plays Program at American Conservatory Theater (Carey Perloff, Artistic Director; Heather Kitchen, Managing Director), San Francisco, California, in August, 1998. It was directed and designed by Craig Slaight; costumes by Callie Floor; lighting and technical direction by Patrick Toebe; the assistant director was Anna Hollenbach; the stage manager was Claire Kendrick. The cast was as follows:

RITA POTTER	Diane Curley
ASA POTTER	Joseph Parks
WARREN POTTER	Justin Okin
JIMMY REEVES	Adam Gerston
JEANNIE LOWELL	Caitlin Talbot

PLAYWRIGHT'S NOTE

When I was just six, I moved with my father, mother, sister, and two brothers from a busy suburb of Manhattan to a tiny, remote town in New Hampshire. It was, even for a girl of six, a cultural shock. My father was a writer of plays and screenplays who valued his solitude, and the town had never experienced someone like him before. He became something of a curiosity, and as the youngest daughter of this curiosity, my peers naturally regarded me with suspicion.

My first few years there were rather lonely ones. In the back of my mind, I always thought we'd be returning to New York. I didn't want to believe that this was a permanent move. And then one day a young woman, newly married, moved onto the farm next to ours. She brought three horses with her, and being a girl who dreamed about horses, I was very keen on meeting her. My mother called her up and asked her if she gave lessons. Thus my "real" life in the tiny town finally began.

Through her I got to know a couple of other young, just married women who'd come to her house in the afternoons and drink a couple of glasses of gin-spiked Kool-Aid (I always drank my Kool-Aid straight) and gossip about the recent happenings in town. Those long, lazy afternoons in her kitchen became firmly embedded in my psyche, only to reinvent themselves years later in my plays.

When They Speak of Rita is the third of my New Hampshire "kitchen" plays. As Craig's actors asked me questions about life in New Hampshire, questions about work and attitudes there, that kitchen slowly began to appear before my eyes again. I often go back to see my friends, spending days, even weeks visiting. However, there was something about the process with Craig and his actors that made those memories fresh and real in a way they hadn't been in years.

When I first spoke to Craig about writing something for him, I had an entirely different play in mind. It was another "kitchen" play, a story about a woman, two teenage boys, a young girl, and some horses. The play is still there, ready to be written. Perhaps when I write it, Craig will let me come back again to work with more of his young actors, allowing me once more to return to the kitchen of my youth.

—*Daisy Foote*

DIRECTOR'S NOTE

"Think three kids (two boys and one girl), ages fourteen, through six-teen, at times on horses at a horse show, watching other events go on. And also think, the mother of the boy and girl, a woman obsessed with men and horses, not necessarily in that order. Two sets, outside the show rink, and the mother's kitchen. There is also a man, I'm not sure if we see him or not, I don't think that we do. He is the mother's new boyfriend that no one likes. Oh, and maybe another character of an uncle who isn't very bright but lives with them as the mother takes care of him."

Thus began the first communication I received, in February of 1998, from Daisy Foote about the commission of a new play for later that year. I had a working meeting with Daisy in Los Angeles in early April to consider the play she had in mind. I think the conversation centered mostly around the stylistic possibilities of having horses on stage without actually having real horses. It didn't matter, I was crazy for Daisy's writing and totally prepared to find a way to realize her vision on stage in our New Plays Program. As it turned out, in May, Daisy called and asked if I would mind terribly if she wrote an altogether different play, one that had come rushing into her mind in recent days, begging to be written…before the horse play. I've learned to never question inspiration. I could tell in the fever-pitch of her voice that this was a burning idea and that we would be onto this play before anything else could be seen. Since I thrive on this kind of energy I said, "We would be happy to have *any* new Daisy Foote play—let it come." Daisy went on to describe a story about a woman who at thirty-seven was having a crisis in her life. This woman was married to a passive husband and together they had one son. There would be two other characters, the son's girlfriend and a male best friend. Through the course of the drama, something would happen (you'll have to read the play) to this small group of people that would explode the normalcy of their quiet New Hampshire existence.

During our early conversations about what would become *When They Speak of Rita*, Daisy talked about the paradigm of young people and adults co-existing in today's world, particularly in the rural sector where the line dividing the social worlds of teens and adults is thinner than in the density of urban culture. Of particular interest to Daisy was the path we take from teen to adult and the compromises along the way. What do we set out to do? What do we end up doing? In the case of Rita (the mother of Daisy's play) the question is even more dramatic, *Why didn't I get any further in my life than this?* Within this painful crossroad would live the drama that Daisy's play would unfold.

By early July, Daisy had the frame of the play complete and sent me a first draft. It was powerful and challenging, an excellent start. We began rehearsals two weeks later, with Daisy in residence—two weeks that saw an amazing transformation of the play into a full and rich drama. Those rehearsals were charged with inspiration from all corners. The actors eagerly embraced new pages with honesty and questions—not doubt or fear, but grabbing for the essential truth in the characters. Daisy was evolving the writing as the actors were simultaneously building their characters—as new pages arrived daily. As Director, I was Daisy's sounding board and the actor's mentor, all the while conceptualizing the physical production.

Most rehearsals ended with playwright and director heading to a local bistro to continue the work. Daisy wrote diligently during time away from rehearsals. In fact I think Daisy did little *but* write during the time she was with us. Indeed the blissful energy of hard work consumed us all. By the end of her residence, we were ready to get to our feet with a deeply defined play and a richness of character that can only be achieved with having the actors involved during the transformative period of the play's rewriting. There was a confidence and a clarity—albeit respectful—to the actor's choices.

The common ground for all of the plays we have commissioned and produced in the New Plays Program is the journey of growing up—a vital human experience that knows no exclusive ownership as we are all on the road toward aging even if we differ about where we are as we pause to consider. In this regard, our plays are at their core *intergenerational.* In Daisy Foote's play, the young people (Warren, Jeannie, and Jimmy) are at an essential crossroad in their lives—*Where do we go after our primary education is complete?* In turn the adults (Rita and Asa) face a reconciliation with where they have come, and the conflict of how to carry on from here. In many respects, the young people in Foote's play became more accomplished than the adults in facing the world head on and stepping into the day. But there is a large part of Rita's complaining and self doubt, and in Asa's simplistic need and crippled communication, that lives in most of our lives, young and old. There is a heartbreaking selfishness that bonds these people even while it places them in conflict with one another. The question, *What will they say about me when I'm gone?,* is timely at *any* age. No matter how we take charge of our lives we all contemplate our contribution somewhere along the road we travel through life's jagged terrain.

When They Speak of Rita moved the adults and the young people in our audience equally. The look back and the look ahead crossed generational lines. The universal question Daisy Foote asks is not easy to answer and challenges us all to genuinely consider the patterns of our past and the responsibilities of our futures.

Now I really must entice Ms. Foote to write that play about the horses. It sounded very exciting.

—*Craig Slaight*

ACTOR'S NOTE

Playing Rita Potter was one of the most exciting, and emotionally trying experiences that I had ever had. I realized that Rita's situation was not uncommon and that it could happen to anyone, most likely a female. As a young woman *When They Speak of Rita* taught me a lot about making choices. Rita's tragedy was that she never made choices for herself, did what she was told, and went along for the ride. She married a man who could not be there for her emotionally, and thought that marriage was making money, reproducing, and keeping clean and fed, basically surviving. Rita was so alone and isolated in her marriage—as an actor this was one of the most uncomfortable roles to play. As Rita, I had virtually no friends on stage, no one to turn to. It was as if I didn't exist and that my only purpose was to keep the coffee brewing, and my family fed, and possibly bring in some money while I was at it. It was painful to live Rita's life, a human being with dreams, hopes, ambitions, and feelings, with no one to support her, just shoot her down. While playing Rita I realized, for me, the most painful part of her life was that she *never* heard the words "I love you" or "thank you" from her family. As a person whose greatest enjoyment comes from the relationships I have with my friends and family, never being acknowledged as a person in this play was extremely lonely. Due to the lack of attention and love Rita received, she felt as though she made no impact on the world, that she served no purpose and that if she disappeared today, no one would care. It is easy to see why Rita would run away with Jimmy, he was the only person who cared about her accomplishments, feelings, and ambitions—all of those things that Warren and Asa never seemed to notice. The most difficult part for me was turning to my husband of twenty years to tell him that I have never been completely happy in our marriage. I do not know if I would be able to do what Rita did, it took an awful lot of strength to be so horribly honest. Probably the saddest part for me was coming out after the show and have all of these tear-filled mothers and wives come to tell me how honestly I had portrayed the part. That means that this happens *everywhere,* to everyone, it is not an isolated or fictional incident. I can not begin to comprehend what these women went through with their lives. Even though we don't know if Rita and Asa ever work things out, I think that there is still an important message. For me, I learned that in life I should not give up my dreams to avoid a little conflict, it's not worth it. Do not be afraid to make choices for yourself, giving up your ambitions is much more painful than enduring a little confrontation.

—*Diane Curley* (Rita)

My friend Justin and I sat dejected on his front porch, our summer hopes all but gone. "There are only five roles in the Daisy Foote play," he told me.

Five parts? Since I started my studies at A.C.T. in the summer of 1995, I had only dreamed of one day performing in a Young Conservatory performance workshop. When I first heard from Craig (the director) about *When They Speak of Rita,* it seemed as if this show might be the one for me. But with only five roles in the play, I couldn't help but feel that my chances of being cast were slim to none.

When I heard that I had been chosen to play Jimmy (and by the way, Justin was cast as well), I literally jumped for joy. I checked my voicemail (almost hourly) at the grocery store where I work, and as soon as I heard Craig's message, I impulsively began running from check-stand to check-stand, periodically leaping into the air to slap five with a fellow co-worker. But this was just the beginning.

I don't think it really hit me until I came to the first rehearsal. We sat around a big table in a big studio (which made me feel very important), all anxious for Craig and Daisy to take us to the Promised Land. But despite this sense of professionalism, everybody was so nice! In essence, I felt welcome to be a part of a new family that would join me on a five-week journey toward artistic excellence.

More than any other part of that first day of rehearsal, I remember Craig saying, "I'm going to direct this play as if it were going to be performed as a main-stage play at the Geary Theater *(the theater in San Francisco where A.C.T.'s professional productions are performed).* I don't know how to talk down to you." Wow. For the first time in my life, I felt as if I were an actor, as if we were all actors, equally committed to our craft and dedicated to help each other create a masterpiece out of Daisy's play. As a result of this tremendous sense of determination, I felt an unprecedented inspiration to create the best character that I could. And so, by the evening after our first rehearsal, I immediately dove into making Daisy's Jimmy a reality.

For me, the "process" as Craig called it, was the most rewarding aspect of my experience in *When They Speak of Rita.* From the first few rehearsals, sitting around a table reading revision after revision, to slowly abandoning the table and walking around a mock set, to finally moving into the theater, I did not feel as if we were preparing a play. Rather, I felt as if we were becoming new people, creating new moments, and building a new reality. Although we rehearsed less than I've ever rehearsed for a play, I felt more relaxed, and less rushed, than I've ever felt in preparing a show for performance. Often, weeks of rehearsal can be a mechanical, meaningless experience. But this was different—cast, director, playwright, technical crew and others brought life and undying commitment to every meeting, determined to do absolute justice to *When They Speak of Rita.*

Of course, this reflection would not be complete if I didn't mention what it was like to work with a living, breathing, tangible playwright. In every other play that I've been in, I've felt as if I had an awkward relationship with the playwright, uncertain as to what was intended for my role or even the show as a whole. But having Daisy Foote there to guide us from the very first meeting brought the rehearsal process to an entirely new level. For once, I was empowered to work with the playwright, not just the playwright's material. In retrospect, I don't know if we could have done it without her.

I could go on forever babbling about why being a part of *When They Speak of Rita* was an unforgettable experience. I talk about the wonderful relationships that I forged, or Craig's hysterical stories about Bobby Lewis, or even about the lovely party that we had at the home of a lady named "Bug." But I'm not going to do that. This experience was so special, so wonderful, and so passionate, that I want to keep some of it to myself. But I will tell you this much: No matter how far I go in theater, I know that I will cherish my experience in *When They Speak of Rita* for as long as I live.

—*Adam Gerston* (Jimmy)

CHARACTERS (in order of appearance)

RITA POTTER: thirty-nine
ASA POTTER: thirty-nine, Rita's husband
WARREN POTTER: nineteen, their son
JIMMY REEVES: nineteen, Warren's best friend
JEANNIE LOWELL: seventeen, Warren's girlfriend

THE SET

The Potter home, Tremont, New Hampshire.

TIME

Late January

When They Speak of Rita

ACT I

SCENE I

We see the kitchen / den and the shed. In the kitchen/den area there is a stove and a refrigerator, a microwave oven, a coffeemaker, and a television. There is a table used for all meals, a couch, and two shabby chairs. There are three exits from the room: The first one is to the stairs up to the second floor of the house, the second is to the hallway leading to the front door of the house, and the third is to the back door. The shed is a workshop/garage where there is a large worktable, parts of engines, and tools for repairing engines. There is an old car seat propped up against a wall. There is one exit from the shed, leading outside. Lights are dimmed on the shed and come up full on the kitchen/den area. Rita Potter (thirty-nine) is preparing dinner. Asa Potter (also thirty-nine) enters the shed, then crosses into the kitchen.

RITA: Hi.

ASA: Jesus it's cold out there. I don't think I remember a colder January.

RITA: You say that every January, Asa.

(A few beats as he drinks his coffee, sniffing.)

ASA: You baking?

RITA: Just put in some cookies.

ASA: Spent all day repairing a hole the size of a crater over to Parker Road.

RITA: Will it hold?

ASA: Doubt it.

RITA: Some lady stopped me at the post office today. I'd never seen her before, but she knew me, knew I was married to you. She wants to know why you don't just pave that road, says she can't keep her car aligned, and at this rate, she'll need a new car in six months.

ASA: What did you say to her?

RITA: What could I say?

ASA: That there's no money in the budget, that as it is—I have to fight for every penny.

RITA: It's not my place to tell her something like that. I'm not the road agent.

ASA: You're the road agent's wife. *(A few beats as he finishes his coffee.)* How's that coffee?

(As she tops it off for him.)

ASA: Warren home yet?

RITA: Called about a half hour ago, said he was just finishing up a job and we shouldn't wait supper for him.

ASA: He's a hard worker—

(A few beats. Rita says nothing.)

ASA: You don't think he is?

RITA: I just wish he would think about college.

ASA: Rita.

RITA: I was hoping that after Jeannie got her scholarship he might change his mind.

ASA: What does that have to do with anything?

RITA: Because she's going to college next year. And if he went to college too, he'd have more in common with her.

ASA: They've known each other since they were babies, how much more in common can you get?

(Rita puts some bread and salad on the table, spoons beef stew into two bowls and serves herself and Asa. They begin eating. A few beats. The door opens, in walks Rita and Asa's son Warren.)

WARREN: Hey.

(As he takes off his coat. Rita goes to get him some stew.)

RITA: *(To Warren.)* Wash your hands.

WARREN: I washed them at Denny's.

RITA: Wash them again.

(He knows there is no arguing with her, washes his hands as she takes his bowl over to the table.)

WARREN: Should have been finished two hours ago, but Denny and me were working on this '92 Toyota. Denny kept saying the problem was in the carburetor. *(Warren gets a beer out of the refrigerator, joins his parents at the table.)* I knew it was the fuel line. *(Eating his stew and drinking his beer.)* Two hours later, we take a look—and surprise surprise—

ASA: A hole.

WARREN: Right down at the bottom. "Well, what do you know about that?" Denny says, like this is the first time he's heard about it. *(A beat.)* And tomorrow, when the customer comes in, Denny will say that *he* figured out the problem, it was all *his* idea, because Denny knows everything. Denny is the guy.

ASA: It is his shop.

WARREN: His shop, his rules, his—stupidity.

(A few long beats. They eat.)

RITA: I went to clean Carol Leon's house this morning. When I got there, she was all upset because this lady who was supposed to do all the food for her sister's baby shower had canceled. And she asks me, "Could you put together a lunch for twelve ladies by one o'clock?" *(A beat.)* I couldn't say no. Poor woman would have jumped off her roof if I had.

ASA: How's that coffee?

(Rita jumps up, pours him more coffee.)

RITA: I made these little crustless sandwiches filled with crabmeat and chopped olives.

WARREN: What the hell kind of sandwich is that?

RITA: A crab salad sandwich. *(A beat.)* Some potato salad and a green salad. And angel food cake with hot fruit compote for dessert.

ASA: Mother's recipe?

RITA: Yes.

ASA: Did you tell them that?

RITA: No.

WARREN: Did she pay you extra?

RITA: She gave me twenty dollars—

WARREN: How many hours did you put into it?

RITA: I don't know, maybe five—

WARREN: Five hours. So that's four dollars an hour. That's less than minimum wage.

ASA: How's that coffee?

(She pours him some more.)

WARREN: So Dad, I've been doing some thinking. Maybe it's time for me to open my own garage.

RITA: And where would you get the money for something like that?

WARREN: Start small. Maybe use the shed—

RITA: Our shed—you want to use our shed.

WARREN: *(To Asa.)* What do you think, Dad?

ASA: It's a big proposition.

RITA: Do something like that, and you can just forget about having time for anything else—

WARREN: What else would I need time for?

RITA: College—

ASA: Rita— *(A beat.)* Give me some time to think about it, Warren.

(Warren gets up from the table.)

WARREN: I need my own garage. Working for a guy like Denny makes it hard for me to live with myself. *(A beat.)* And if you think it's something you don't want to do, I'm going to ask Jeannie's father about using his barn. *(He heads for the back door.)* Jimmy's coming over, we're working on that truck he just bought.

ASA: I thought you told him not to buy it.

WARREN: He didn't listen.

RITA: Is Jeannie stopping by?

WARREN: No. She's got some paper due tomorrow.

RITA: She's a good student.

(Warren exits through the back door.)

RITA: But then I guess that's why she got a full scholarship for college. *(Rita opens the oven, takes out a tray of cookies, and puts them on a rack to cool.)* I really did enjoy cooking that lunch today. It's something I wouldn't mind trying again.

ASA: Next time you'll know to ask for more money.

RITA: Are you going to let him use the shed?

ASA: What do you think?

RITA: As if what I had to say would matter—you've already made up your mind.

ASA: I have not.

RITA: You're going to let him do it, I know you. You always give in to him.

ASA: I think he'll do well with it. He's a hard worker, and he knows his cars. *(Getting up.)* I'm going upstairs.

RITA: Are you feeling sick?

ASA: My head—an ache behind my eyes. *(He goes up the stairs.)*

(Rita turns on the radio. She finds an oldies station and begins singing along with a song from her high school days. She is like a singer onstage, swaying to the music and belting out the lyrics. She continues to sing as she clears the table. Jimmy Reeves, Warren's best friend, enters from the hallway to the front door. Rita immediately stops singing and turns down the radio.)

JIMMY: Sounding good, Mrs. Potter. Sounding wicked good.

RITA: Oh be quiet, Jimmy.

JIMMY: I'm serious, you could be one of them backup singers.

RITA: Just a backup singer?

JIMMY: *(Laughing.)* You'd be the leader of the pack. Guys tearing off their underwear and throwing it at your feet.

RITA: Are you hungry, Jimmy?

JIMMY: I can always eat.

(She serves him some stew. He sits down and starts to eat.)

JIMMY: Jesus this is good.

RITA: It's just Crock Pot.

JIMMY: Take your Crock Pot any day.

(A few beats as he eats and she pours herself some coffee, sits down across from him.)

RITA: I catered a lunch for Carol Leon today.

JIMMY: Oh yuh—and how was that?

RITA: Do you know what that means?

JIMMY: Uhhhhhhh— (Laughing.) No, I guess I don't.

RITA: It's when you go into someone's house and cook a meal for them.

JIMMY: You mean like a chef?

RITA: That's part of it. But the cooking you're doing is usually for some sort of party, like a birthday or a wedding, or like what I did today, lunch for a baby shower. And you might even provide the silverware or the plates and even do some of the theme planning and the decorating.

JIMMY: Did you do any of that?

RITA: No, just the cooking—it was a last-minute thing. Her caterer canceled, and she asked me to fill in.

JIMMY: I bet you did a good job.

RITA: I did all right.

JIMMY: No one can cook like you, Mrs. Potter. I don't see you heating up frozen foods in the microwave and calling them breakfast, lunch, and dinner.

RITA: Your mother?

JIMMY: The frozen stuff—that's her idea of a home-cooked meal.

RITA: Did I ever tell you how she burned her sugar cookies? (A beat.) Our freshman year in Home Ec—your mother was the only one who burned the bottom of her sugar cookies.

JIMMY: Can't say that I'm surprised.

RITA: But she was very popular. Both her and your father. Queen and King of the Junior and Senior Proms—

(Jimmy has finished his stew.)

RITA: Do you want some more?

JIMMY: I think I'm good.

(She takes his plate over to the sink.)

RITA: How about some cookies? Peanut Butter Butterscotch.

(Jimmy thinks about it.)

RITA: Hot out of the oven.

JIMMY: I guess I could try a few.

(She is putting some cookies on a plate.)

JIMMY: Did you and Mr. Potter go to the party at the town hall last night?

(She gives him the cookies.)

RITA: No, we never go to those parties.

JIMMY: I guess I knew that.

RITA: That's not our crowd, not that we have a crowd.

JIMMY: And who needs a crowd when you've got your family—that should be enough.

RITA: Were your parents there?

JIMMY: What do you think? (A beat.) I was with the twins. When Ma and Dad got home, they were both wicked drunk. Ma was screaming at Dad for dancing with all the other ladies except her. (A beat.) Hey—I know my Dad's no angel. (A beat.) But maybe if she got her act together. Started cooking some decent meals, lost some weight—he might stop looking around. (A beat.) I see pictures of her when she was younger, she had a nice body then.

RITA: Yes she did.

JIMMY: That was the woman my Dad fell in love with. Not the fat lady always nagging at him. (A beat.) These cookies are wicked good.

(Rita indicates the plate.)

RITA: Have some more.

(He takes another.)

JIMMY: And the thing I really hate is when they try and make me take sides—

RITA: But you don't do that?

JIMMY: No, of course not. (A beat.) But now that I'm working with my Dad, all he wants to do is complain about her all day long. What a bitch I have for a mother, and if it weren't for the twins being so young, he'd be out the door tomorrow.

RITA: Maybe you should get another job—

JIMMY: Doing what?

RITA: Jimmy, you're nineteen. There's a world of possibilities out there.

JIMMY: I couldn't—My Dad, he would have a fit if I quit. He's training me to be his partner. And someday when he retires, the business will be mine.

RITA: Is that what you want?

JIMMY: I don't know. (A beat.) I just know that I can't be away from the twins. Everything just keeps getting worse with Ma and Dad and the twins really need me.

RITA: What about college?

JIMMY: Me—college? I don't think so. I know my limits, and I'm not smart like Jeannie, I know that.

(*Warren bursts into the kitchen.*)

WARREN: What the hell are you doing?

JIMMY: What the hell does it look like I'm doing?

WARREN: I thought you wanted your truck fixed.

RITA: He was hungry.

WARREN: He's always hungry. (*Looking around the room.*) Where's Dad?

RITA: He said he had a headache, he went upstairs to rest.

WARREN: Is he sick?

RITA: He just said it was an ache behind his eyes.

(*Jimmy gets himself some coffee.*)

JIMMY: My Dad wanted me to pass a message on to him. Tell him that no matter what happens he'll always have his vote for road agent. You won't catch my Dad voting for no stranger.

WARREN: What are you talking about?

JIMMY: You don't know about it?

WARREN: Know about what?

JIMMY: That guy from Silicon Valley, the one who bought the old Bennett farm. Me and Dad are doing all his rewiring. He told us that he was planning on running for road agent in March.

WARREN: (*To Rita.*) Did you know about this?

RITA: No.

JIMMY: I'm sure it will be fine, just some rich guy flapping his wings.

(*Warren has heard enough. He goes to the door, turns.*)

WARREN: Are you coming?

JIMMY: Yeah, sure. (*A beat.*) Thanks for the food, Mrs. Potter.

(*She smiles. Jimmy follows Warren out the back door. Rita goes back to her dishes. Asa comes into the kitchen again.*)

ASA: Was that Jimmy I heard?

RITA: I gave him something to eat. He's practically starving half the time. (*A beat.*) How's your head?

ASA: Better. (*He sits down in front of the television, turns it on.*)

RITA: Asa, do you know anything about this guy from California running against you for road agent?

ASA: I've heard something about it.

RITA: Why didn't you tell me?

(*He says nothing.*)

RITA: Asa.

ASA: There was nothing to tell.

RITA: Nothing to tell? No one has ever run against you before. What if he wins?

ASA: He's not going to win.

RITA: Maybe you should think about a campaign. I could make some signs, "Re-elect Asa Potter for Road Agent."

ASA: No.

RITA: It's a good idea.

ASA: Rita.

RITA: I'll take charge of everything.

ASA: *(Yelling.)* I said no!

(She pulls back, realizing that he is serious.)

ASA: Now why did you make me do that? You know I don't like it. *(A beat.)* He's just some guy from California, retired early—now he's got too much time on his hands.

(He continues watching television. Rita finishes her dishes. Jeannie Lowell, Warren's girlfriend, enters from the hallway to the front door.)

RITA: I thought you had a paper to write?

JEANNIE: I finished early.

RITA: What was it for?

JEANNIE: English, Mr. Collins.

RITA: I hated writing papers for him. He was always on me about my grammar.

ASA: I bet Jeannie doesn't have to worry about that.

RITA: I wouldn't think so. She's the smartest girl in the school.

JEANNIE: No, I'm not.

RITA: A full scholarship to the University of New Hampshire. How many other kids in your class have one of these? Not one.

(Asa gets up.)

ASA: I think I'll poke my head into the shed, see how the wars are going.

JEANNIE: Can you tell him I'm here?

ASA: I can. *(He goes out the back door.)*

RITA: Have you heard anything about this man from California running against Asa?

JEANNIE: No.

RITA: Jimmy told us about him tonight. No one's ever run against Asa before. And I thought we might try starting a campaign, make some signs, come up with some slogans. But Asa says he won't do it. *(A beat.)* What do you think?

JEANNIE: I don't think anyone will vote for the guy.

RITA: I'm not so sure about that. We don't know half the town anymore. They have no loyalty to Asa. *(A beat.)* I've got some cookies.

JEANNIE: No thanks.

RITA: Peanut Butter Butterscotch.

JEANNIE: I'm not hungry.

RITA: What does eating one of my cookies hot out of the oven have to do with being hungry?

(Jeannie bursts into tears.)

RITA: Jeannie—what on earth—

JEANNIE: My dad tonight, Rita—he was crying. In the kitchen at the table, drinking coffee and crying like a baby.

RITA: Did you ask him about it?

JEANNIE: God no. He didn't even know I was there. Thought I was still upstairs doing my paper. *(A beat.)* I think he's wicked freaked out about me going to college in the fall. I don't know what he'll do without me.

RITA: He'll survive.

JEANNIE: But he's never been without me before. Ever since Ma died, it's been him and me. Now he'll be all alone.

RITA: Stop being so dramatic.

JEANNIE: I'm not! I'm worried about my dad!

RITA: Your father wants you to go to college. It's a dream come true for him.

JEANNIE: I guess.

RITA: I know. *(A beat.)* Every time I see him in town he grabs me and says, "Can you believe our Jeannie is going to college on a full scholarship in the fall?" I'm so proud of her. *(A beat.)* And he's going to be a little sad, that's perfectly normal. But it doesn't mean that you should stay home, sacrifice everything— *(A few beats.)* You sure you don't want a cookie?

JEANNIE: All right, maybe just one.

(Rita gives her two.)

RITA: Take two.

(Jeannie eats one of them.)

RITA: It's going to be fine, Jeannie. You'll start school, your dad will adjust, and life will go on.

(A few beats. Rita takes a cookie too.)

RITA: You know what I did today? I catered a lunch for twelve ladies at Carol Leon's. Her caterer canceled so she asked me to do it.

JEANNIE: Is that a good thing?

RITA: It is when you spend your day scrubbing other people's toilets. *(A beat.)* And you think about that. You think about me cleaning houses every time you worry about going away to college. When you finish, you'll have a college degree and you won't ever have to do that.

JEANNIE: You don't have to clean houses, Rita. There are other things you could do.

RITA: Like what?

JEANNIE: How about this catering deal?

RITA: Oh it's not something I could ever do seriously.

JEANNIE: Why not?

RITA: Because I've tried to start other businesses. You know I have. And you know that nothing has ever worked. I've always had to go back to cleaning houses. *(A beat.)* But when a person has a college education, they have all sorts of choices. The world is an open book.

(A few beats. They munch their cookies.)

JEANNIE: What about Warren? Do you think he'll miss me?

(Lights dim on the kitchen/den. Lights come up full on the shed. We hear Warren and Jimmy offstage.)

WARREN: Tighten this one over here. *(A beat.)* And let's connect this over here— *(A beat.)* Now give it a try.

(We hear an attempt to start the motor, it doesn't quite turn over.)

WARREN: Okay, I think I know what it is. *(A beat.)* Get me that Philips' head— *(A beat.)* This should do it. *(A beat.)* And one more time.

(This time the truck starts.)

JIMMY: All right!

(The boys appear.)

JIMMY: You're a genius.

WARREN: Shut up.

JIMMY: A goddamn genius for engines.

(They go over to a cooler and take out some beers, open them, and drink.)

WARREN: Let's see if it keeps running. I don't trust that piece of shit.

JIMMY: I'm not worried.

(They drink.)

WARREN: So I asked my dad about opening a garage in the shed.

JIMMY: What did he say?

WARREN: Said he had to think about it. But I think he might let me do it, unless Ma gives him a hard time.

JIMMY: Why would she do that?

WARREN: Because that's what she does.

JIMMY: Your ma's good people.

WARREN: You don't have to live with her.

JIMMY: No, you don't have to live with *my* ma.

WARREN: We're both nineteen and out of school, aren't we supposed to be living on our own? *(A beat.)* So what's the deal with this California guy?

JIMMY: Made a killing in computers, retired early, moved to town.

WARREN: What the hell does he want to be road agent for?

JIMMY: Says to me and Dad that the roads are crap, and it's all *your* dad's fault. Says he's behind the times.

WARREN: And what the hell did you say?

JIMMY: I'm working for the guy, Warren. He's handing me and my Dad a fat check every week. It's not like I can tell him that he's full of shit. *(A beat.)* But we won't vote for him, I can tell you that.
(They drink.)

JIMMY: You want to know something else about this California guy? *(A beat.)* My Dad's screwing his wife.

WARREN: How do you know?

JIMMY: Last Friday when we finally finished the job, the California guy offered us some beers for a job well done. The wife was there too, and she kept looking over at my Dad. I know that look— *(A beat.)* And this guy, this California guy, he keeps talking. How there's nothing like small town living, nothing like it at all—
(Both boys start to laugh. Asa enters the shed.)

ASA: How's it going?

WARREN: Problem solved.

ASA: Was that before or after the beer?

JIMMY: I gotta go. Pick the twins up at a friend's house. *(Pointing to Warren.)* Your son's a genius, Mr. Potter—a genius for engines.
(He exits, we hear his truck start, back out, drive away.)

ASA: Wish you wouldn't drink down here, Warren.

WARREN: Just a couple of beers.

ASA: That may be. But if you're going to open a shop in my shed, I'll ask you to live by my rules. No alcohol.

WARREN: You mean I can do it?

ASA: I don't see why not.

WARREN: You don't know what this means to me. Something I've wanted to do since I was—Jesus—I don't know, for as long as I can remember.

ASA: I know.

WARREN: Can't pay you a lot of money right now.

ASA: Save your money. Just get yourself on your feet first. *(A beat.)* Jeannie's in the kitchen, she finished her paper early. Are you going to be here awhile?

WARREN: I've got some cleaning up to do.

ASA: Then I'll send her down. *(Asa starts to leave.)*

WARREN: Dad.

(He stops.)

WARREN: You won't regret this. They'll be lining up for me to fix their cars.

(Asa exits. Warren goes over to his table, starts putting things away. A few beats. Jeannie enters, coming up behind him and putting her hands over his ears. She kisses the back of his neck.)

JEANNIE: Guess who.

WARREN: Is that you, Ma?

(She pulls away.)

JEANNIE: That's disgusting.

(They kiss.)

JEANNIE: Dad's going down to Aunt Clara's this weekend, we'll have the whole house to ourselves.

WARREN: I got better news than that.

JEANNIE: What could be better than that?

WARREN: My dad said I can use the shed for my garage.

JEANNIE: Oh my God, that's great—

WARREN: Dream come true. And you can help me run it.

JEANNIE: I can help get it started. But I'll be in school next year.

WARREN: Forget about college, help me run the garage.

JEANNIE: Warren.

WARREN: You can go to school at night.

JEANNIE: No I can't, I have a scholarship, which means I have to live on campus and go to school full-time. That's how it is, and we both should start getting used to it.

(A few beats. We see Rita approaching with cookies and sodas. She hesitates when she hears their raised voices. They don't see her in the shadows.)

JEANNIE: Right after Ma died, everyone wanted me to get away, so Aunt Clara and Uncle Ben took me to Disney World. I cried the whole time I was there, I just wanted to go home and see my dad, but everyone kept saying that it was better for me to be at Disney World. I'd be in the hotel room when Dad would call from home, and I'd hear Aunt Clara say to him, "She's having a wicked good time, the time of her life." She wouldn't let me talk to him. She didn't want him to know that I was upset. It was horrible.

WARREN: So what are you saying?

JEANNIE: When I'm away at school, I don't want to be sad all the time. How am I ever going to get through four years if all I ever am is sad about being away from you?

WARREN: You'll get up there, be around a lot of other guys and you'll forget about me.

JEANNIE: No I won't.

WARREN: How do you know?

JEANNIE: I just do. And you better start trusting me, or we don't stand a chance.

(Warren nods. They kiss again. Rita slips out of the shed. Now Warren pulls her onto the car seat, begins to kiss her.)

JEANNIE: What are you doing?

(He smiles, continuing to kiss her.)

JEANNIE: What if your ma and dad come down here?

WARREN: They won't. We'll keep it really quiet.

JEANNIE: I don't think this is a good idea.

WARREN: Sshhh, sshhhh.

(As they continue to kiss, lights come down.)

SCENE II

Three months later. The middle of April. Lights come up full on the Potter kitchen / den. Rita, shaking snow off her coat, enters from the front hallway. She is carrying a large plastic shopping bag. She takes off her coat, dumps the contents of the bag on the table. Out comes heavy card stock paper, magic markers, pencils, rulers, scissors and a book. She picks the book up and reads its title aloud.

RITA: "How to Start Your Very Own Catering Business" *(She leafs through the book, then puts it aside.)* First, I need a name. *(She starts scribbling names down on a piece of paper.)* "Rita's Catering," too boring. *(Writing another name.)* "Rita's Secret Delights." I don't think so. *(She thinks for a few moments, then...)* Oh, I know.

(As she is writing this one down on the paper, Jimmy comes into the room from the front hallway, brushing off the snow.)

JIMMY: Not fit for man or beast out there. *(He takes off his coat.)* A real spring storm. *(Jimmy sits down at the table.)* Me and Dad decided to knock off early, no point trying to navigate. That California guy don't know the first thing about keeping the roads clear.

RITA: But that's who people voted for.

JIMMY: Well, now they're paying for it.

RITA: How does this sound to you, Jimmy? "Delectable Edibles by Rita."

JIMMY: Sounds good.

RITA: Do you know what it's for?

JIMMY: No.

RITA: It's the name of my new catering business, "Delectable Edibles by Rita."

JIMMY: Are you starting a business?

RITA: You bet I am, that's why I have all these materials. I'm going to make some cards and signs, let people know about it.

JIMMY: I'll take some of those cards, pass them out to customers.

RITA: All right. *(A beat.)* Would you like some coffee?

JIMMY: Sure. *(A beat.)* Things have been sad and gloomy around here lately. It's nice to see you so up again.

(Rita is making the coffee.)

RITA: Well I do feel up. I feel on top of the world. *(A beat.)* No more moping around. No more worrying about Asa not having a job. I'm starting a catering business and it's going to be a huge success.

JIMMY: There you go.

RITA: How about some cherry pie?

JIMMY: Sounds good.

(Rita takes some pie out of the refrigerator.)

RITA: With some ice cream on it?

JIMMY: Even better.

(She puts the ice cream on the pie.)

RITA: I never thought that doing something I love could actually make me money. Even after I cooked the lunch for Carol Leon and did a good job with it, I didn't really think it was possible.

JIMMY: So when did you realize?

RITA: This morning.

JIMMY: This morning?

RITA: It didn't start out like that. At first I was feeling all depressed about Asa still not having a job, wondering if maybe I should find some more houses to clean. I wanted to pull the covers over my head, tell the world to go away.

JIMMY: But you didn't.

RITA: But I did roll over for more sleep, and just as I closed my eyes, it came to me—

(Jimmy takes a bite of his pie.)

JIMMY: The proof is in the pie.

(Warren comes in from the back door.)

WARREN: Hey Ma, you got some coffee going? *(He sees Jimmy.)* What are you doing here?

JIMMY: Dad and I decided to knock off early with the snow.

WARREN: That's what you told your customers?

JIMMY: No one expects us in this weather.

(Warren pours himself some coffee.)

RITA: You want some pie?

WARREN: Just coffee, I've still got work to do.

JIMMY: That California guy doesn't know the first thing about snow removal. Cars are off the road all over the place. Someone's gonna get hurt. *(A beat.)* People are going to be real sorry they voted Mr. Potter out of office.

(Warren sees the stuff on the table.)

WARREN: What's all this?

RITA: "Rita's Delectable Edibles."

JIMMY: Your ma's new business.

RITA: My house-cleaning days will soon be a thing of the past. I'm going to be a full-time caterer. *(A beat.)* I'm going to hand out cards, put up signs. And let all the people I'm cleaning for, let them know about it.

JIMMY: Then once you get your first customer, they'll tell people, and then they'll tell people. Before you know it, you'll be working all the time.

RITA: Caterers can make very good money, a lot more than I'm making now.

WARREN: How much did all this stuff cost you?

RITA: What stuff?

WARREN: All these supplies and the book, it must have cost you something.

RITA: It's nothing you have to concern yourself with.

WARREN: Dad still doesn't have a job.

RITA: I can't start a business unless I'm willing to spend some money first.

WARREN: You don't have the money to spend.

RITA: Oh I see you can have dreams, but I can't have mine.

WARREN: I'm just talking about being realistic, Ma. *(A beat.)* You clean houses. And that's how people see you.

JIMMY: I don't think that's true. Not at all.

WARREN: Who the hell asked you?

(Jeannie, shaking off snow, enters the kitchen.)

JEANNIE: I hate it when it snows this time of year. You're all psyched for spring. The crocuses are blooming, the ladyslippers are popping, then all this happens. *(She stops, picking up on the tension.)*

(The lights begin flickering.)

JIMMY: Looks like we might lose our power. *(A beat.)* Better get going. *(A beat.)* Thanks for the pie and coffee, Mrs. Potter. *(He goes out the front hallway.)*

(The power goes off. They are now in the dark.)

RITA: There it goes. *(She fumbles in a drawer, finds a flashlight, turns it on. Then she finds another one, hands it to Warren.)* Are you going to need any candles?

WARREN: Can't use candles in the shed, might set something off. *(He is heading for the back door, looks back at Jeannie.)* You coming?

JEANNIE: *(To Rita.)* Are you okay?

RITA: Of course.

(Jeannie follows Warren through the back door. Rita finds some candles, lights them. She sits at the table, reads more of her new book. Jeannie and Warren enter the shed.)

WARREN: Let's see if we can find that power light, it's buried around here somewhere.

(They look around the room.)

JEANNIE: Did you and your mother have a fight?

(He's still looking.)

JEANNIE: When I walked into the kitchen, the two of you looked like you might kill each other.

(He finds the power light, turns it on.)

WARREN: Dad's out of a job, and she goes out and buys about fifty dollars worth of crap on some business she's thinking about starting. Catering. *(A beat.)* Where the hell does she come up with these ideas? One year it's the Christmas wreaths, gonna make tons of money making Christmas wreaths. Goes and spends all this cash on supplies. Makes me and Dad go into the wood to cut pine boughs, then we have to twist all the wire for her too. My hands were bleeding from twisting so much wire. And

after making about a hundred of those things, you know how many she
sold?

JEANNIE: I know.

WARREN: Two. One to you and the other to Jimmy. *(A beat.)* And let's not forget the home bakery "Rita's Pies and Cakes."

JEANNIE: All right.

WARREN: And the time she thought the town could use a tiny tot's birthday
party planner, and she went out and bought the clown suit and all those
party games.

JEANNIE: I'm pregnant.

(Warren turns to her. He has no words.)

JEANNIE: I'm going to have a baby.

(Lights come down.)

SCENE III

*Early the next morning. Lights come up full on the kitchen/den. Rita enters
from the stairs, starts coffee. Warren enters from the stairs.*

RITA: Warren, your father never came home last night. I went to bed around
ten. I heard you come in later, but your father never came in. Should we
call the police?

WARREN: No, I'll take a drive around, maybe he just got into something.

RITA: Your father? What would your father ever get into? *(A beat.)* Do you
want to take a cup of coffee?

WARREN: All right.

(She takes a cup out of the cupboard. Asa enters from the front hallway.)

ASA: Morning.

RITA: Where have you been?

ASA: Pulling cars out of ditches.

RITA: Whose cars?

ASA: Half the town. The roads haven't been plowed, never mind sanded, and
cars were piling up. *(A beat.)* How's that coffee?

(He sits down, and she pours coffee for him and Warren.)

ASA: I found one lady over to Grady Hill, her car spun out and went into a
ditch. She's got two babies in the car with her. She was about to run out
of gas when I found her. *(A beat.)* The babies are screaming and crying.

She's as white as a ghost and shaking all over, said she'd left her cell phone at home. And she couldn't leave the car, couldn't leave the babies. *(A beat.)* So I piled everyone into the truck and drove them home.

RITA: Who was she?

ASA: New in town, I forget her name.

WARREN: She probably voted for the California guy.

ASA: We don't know that.

WARREN: What was she driving?

ASA: A Volvo station wagon.

WARREN: She voted for him. *(A beat.)* I thought about waiting a week or so, but I don't see the point. Now's as good a time as any. *(A beat.)* Jeannie and I are getting married. Right after she graduates in June.

RITA: What about her college?

WARREN: She's not going, or at least she's not going now. Maybe in a few years, part-time or nights.

RITA: But she has the full scholarship.

WARREN: She'll give it back.

RITA: She's pregnant.

WARREN: You breathe a word of that to anyone, Ma—you breathe a goddamn word—

RITA: As if people aren't going to figure it out.

ASA: Let's not talk about this now. Get on with the day, tonight when we're calmer we can talk about it over supper.

WARREN: There's nothing to talk about. Jeannie and I are getting married. *(He gets up to top off his coffee.)* And I won't be home for supper, I'll be at Jeannie's house. We're breaking the news to her father.

RITA: I'm sure he'll have a thing or two to say about it.

(He walks out the back door.)

RITA: I want to hear Jeannie's side of this. I can't believe that this is something she really wants.

ASA: She's pregnant. That changes everything.

RITA: It doesn't have to. She could have an abortion.

ASA: Rita.

RITA: And if she doesn't want to do that, she could have the baby, give it up for adoption and start college in January.

ASA: You're talking about our grandchild.

RITA: I'm thirty-nine years old, Asa. What could a grandchild possibly mean to me? *(A beat.)* Her poor father, he was so proud of her and that scholarship.

The first Lowell to ever go to college. Maybe he can talk some sense into her.

ASA: Maybe she doesn't want to go to college.

RITA: Don't be ridiculous, of course she does. It's always been her dream. *(Rita is serving him his breakfast.)*

ASA: I'll need to get back out there soon. Make sure I'm not needed.

RITA: It's not snowing anymore.

ASA: But the roads still haven't been cleared. Some people might need their driveways plowed or a car pulled out of a snow bank. *(A beat.)* You should have seen it, Rita. Snow piling up, and no one there to remove it. You could see the fear in people's eyes, wondering where the hell the plows and sanders were. It was terrible, just terrible.

RITA: It's not your problem anymore.

ASA: How can you say that?

RITA: They voted for someone else.

ASA: But all I know is roads. *(A beat.)* I joined my father's crew when I was eighteen. And when he died and the town elected me, I was the youngest road agent in the history of Tremont. *(A beat.)* Of course it's my problem if it has to do with roads. Of course it is. *(Asa sees Rita's catering book on the table. Picking it up.)* What's this?

RITA: It's for my new business.

ASA: What new business?

RITA: My new catering business. "Rita's Delectable Edibles."

ASA: Come again?

RITA: That's what I'm calling it, "Rita's Delectable Edibles." *(Indicating the book.)* The book tells me everything I need to know about getting started.

(He turns the book over.)

ASA: Twenty-five dollars. This book cost twenty-five dollars.

RITA: It tells me everything I need to know.

ASA: You'll need to take it back, Rita.

RITA: Why?

ASA: We can't afford twenty-five dollars. Jesus, Rita…we barely have anything left in our savings, and you're spending twenty-five dollars on some book.

RITA: It's not just some book.

ASA: You'll need to take it back. *(A beat. He stands up.)* I don't know if I'll be home for lunch. Depends on what I find out there.

RITA: Don't you want breakfast?

ASA: Grab some on the road. *(He leans in, kisses her on the cheek.)* See you later, grandmother.

RITA: Don't call me that.

ASA: It's a fact. You better get used to it. *(He goes out the front door.)*
(Rita is just standing in the middle of the room. She goes slowly over to the sink to finish the dishes. Lights down.)

SCENE IV

A week later. The lights come up full on the shed. Jeannie is sitting on the car seat, reading Bride's *magazine. Rita calls from offstage.*

RITA: Warren, my car's making a funny noise—Warren? *(Rita enters the shed, carrying two bags of groceries. She is surprised to see Jeannie.)*

JEANNIE: He's not here, he and Jimmy went into town to try and find a part for Jimmy's truck.

RITA: It's broken again? *(She puts the bags down.)*

JEANNIE: Warren told him not to buy it.

RITA: My car's making a grinding noise, it started about two miles from the house.

JEANNIE: Warren will fix it.

RITA: I hope so, I know we can't afford a new car. *(A beat.)* What are you reading?

JEANNIE: Nothing, just a magazine.
(Rita leans over to see the title.)

RITA: *Brides*—
(Jeannie shrugs.)

RITA: Are you planning a big wedding?

JEANNIE: No, not big, but something nice.

RITA: Would you like some help with it?

JEANNIE: I wouldn't think you'd want to do that, you're probably really mad at me.

RITA: Is that why I haven't seen you in over a week, you thought I was mad at you?
(Jeannie shrugs again.)

RITA: I left a message with your father, did you get it?

JEANNIE: Yes.

RITA: Why didn't you call me back?

JEANNIE: Because I didn't want you yelling at me. I've gotten enough of that from Dad.

RITA: Well, you can't really blame him, Jeannie. Every time I ran into him at the post office, he'd say—

JEANNIE: I know, how proud he was of me.

(A few beats.)

RITA: How far along are you?

JEANNIE: Three months.

RITA: So there's still time.

JEANNIE: For what?

RITA: Don't tell me you haven't thought about it.

JEANNIE: No, I haven't. And you should be ashamed of yourself for even mentioning it.

RITA: You're just going to give it all up, everything you've worked so hard for.

JEANNIE: It's the right thing to do. And I'm happy, happier than I've been in a long time.

RITA: For about five minutes. Talk to me next year when the novelty of marriage and baby has worn off. You'll start to think about that scholarship and wonder why you ever gave it up.

JEANNIE: I don't think so. I don't think I ever wanted to go to college.

RITA: Then why on earth did you apply for a scholarship?

JEANNIE: Because everyone kept telling me to do it. *(A beat.)* But the whole time I was thinking about Warren, wondering how I could ever leave him for four years.

RITA: So you went and got pregnant?

JEANNIE: I don't want to talk about this anymore. I'm sorry if you're disappointed in me. But this is how things are, so start dealing with it.

(Jimmy and Warren enter the shed.)

JEANNIE: Did you find what you needed?

JIMMY: Only if it works.

JEANNIE: It'll work.

WARREN: How do you know that? *(A beat.)* We try the part and it doesn't work, that's it. I'm not wasting anymore time on this piece of crap I told you not to buy.

RITA: Warren, my car's making a funny noise, a kind of grinding sound.

WARREN: Is it the brake pads?

RITA: No, it's something different, something I've never heard before.

WARREN: I'll try to get to it tonight.

RITA: Thank you. *(A beat.)* I'm going to start supper. *(Taking one of the bags of groceries, she exits into the kitchen. She takes off her coat and begins putting away the groceries.)*

JEANNIE: *(To Warren.)* Can you give me a ride home now? Aunt Clara and Uncle Ben are coming up tonight, and I have to be at the house waiting for them.

WARREN: Are you sure you want to do that?

JEANNIE: Dad says I have to tell them, and I have to cook supper.

(They start out together, Warren turns back to Jimmy.)

WARREN: I'll be right back, don't touch anything while I'm gone.

(They exit. Rita goes out the back door and re-enters the shed.)

JIMMY: Warren's running Jeannie home.

RITA: *(Going to get the other bag of groceries.)* Forgot my other bag.

JIMMY: Let me help you with that, Mrs. Potter. *(He picks the bag up.)*

RITA: Thank you, Jimmy. *(She leads the way out of the shed.)*

(Lights dim on the shed, come up full on the kitchen/den. Rita and Jimmy come in.)

JIMMY: So it's big news about Jeannie and Warren— *(He puts the groceries on the table.)* You're going to be a grandma. *(A beat.)* You sure don't look like a grandma. You and Jeannie could be sisters.

(Rita laughs.)

JIMMY: I mean it.

RITA: Can I make you a cup of coffee?

JIMMY: I wouldn't say no.

RITA: And a piece of pie with it?

JIMMY: You read my mind.

(She is putting on the coffee and getting him the pie.)

JIMMY: Marriage—and children—that's a big deal. But then I've never had much luck with the girls. I've never even had a girlfriend.

RITA: They're not ready for this.

JIMMY: You don't think so? I don't know…they seem pretty psyched about it, making a lot of plans.

(She gives him his pie, he takes a bite.)

JIMMY: Of course my parents thought they were ready for marriage too. And look what happened to them. I look at pictures of them when they were younger, they look pretty happy. Ma's about thirty pounds thinner, and Dad's looking at her like she's the girl of his dreams— *(A beat.)* I guess that's just how it goes, you never know what the future holds.

(A few beats of silence.)

RITA: When I was in high school, I think it was my senior year—we learned about something called brown dwarves...

JIMMY: Brown dwarves?

RITA: It's a star that is no longer burning, a dead star. *(A beat.)* I think I'm a brown dwarf, Jimmy.

JIMMY: No...

RITA: It's true. *(A beat.)* Only I think I've always been a brown dwarf. Always to be a brown dwarf, never a star.

JIMMY: Don't you say that. Why do you think I come over here all the time?

RITA: Your truck's broken. You and Warren are friends, and he can fix it.

JIMMY: Maybe that's how it used to be, but not anymore. *(A beat.)* That truck is never gonna be fixed, I know that. And I'm glad. One more reason for me to come over here. One more reason for me to see you.

RITA: Jimmy—

JIMMY: I can't stop thinking about you. When I'm at work with my Dad, when I'm at my house, when I'm in my truck. When I'm sleeping, when I'm sleeping I'm dreaming about you. And you're a star in my dreams, Mrs. Potter, just like you're a star when I'm awake, a bright, shining star. *(A beat.)* It's your family, they're the ones making you feel this way. They don't appreciate you. I see the way Warren yells at you, I see it and I can't stand it. It's all I can do not to punch him out. *(A beat.)* I love you, Rita—I love you. *(He grabs her, kisses her. Then he pulls away.)* I'm sorry, I'm sorry—

(She pulls him back to her. They are in each other's arms. The lights go down.)

END OF ACT I

ACT II

SCENE I

Three months later. July. Lights come up full on the kitchen/den. Jeannie, now noticeably pregnant, opens the oven door.

JEANNIE: *(To the oven.)* Don't burn, don't burn. *(She closes the oven, stirs something on top of the stove, turns to set the table.)*
(Asa comes into the kitchen from the front hallway.)
ASA: Hiya—
JEANNIE: Supper should be ready in about half an hour, I've got a shortcake in the oven.
ASA: Sounds good. *(A beat.)* How's that coffee?
JEANNIE: Oh jeez—I forgot, just give me a second.
ASA: Don't rush.
JEANNIE: But I know how you like your coffee when you get home. *(A beat.)* So how was your day?
ASA: Not bad. I was over to Parker Road, the California guy's having it paved.
JEANNIE: I saw that.
ASA: For years I tried to get money from the town to do that. And they wouldn't hear it. *(A beat.)* Now this guy, in charge just these five months, and he's paving roads and buying new equipment.
JEANNIE: I heard he's using his own money.
ASA: I don't believe that. I think he's just very good at the political side of things. For me it was being out on the roads, being hands-on. But when it came to appearing before the selectmen or the budget committee, my mouth would go all thick and furry. I sounded like an idiot.
JEANNIE: You were the best road agent this town has ever known.
ASA: I don't know about that.
JEANNIE: I do.
ASA: This guy, this California guy deserves some credit. After a rough start this spring he seems to be turning it around, seems to be making his mark. *(Sniffing.)* Is something burning?
JEANNIE: Oh jeez— *(She opens the oven, takes out the charred remains of her shortcake.)*
ASA: That's too bad.
(Jeannie throws it in the sink.)
JEANNIE: I've never been much of a baker.

ASA: There are worse things. *(A beat.)* Rita liked to bake.

JEANNIE: She was really good at it, her pies and cakes—

ASA: Did you use her shortcake recipe?

JEANNIE: The exact same one. I'm sorry.

ASA: What do you have to be sorry for? With everything you do around here, cooking, cleaning house, never mind what you're doing with Warren's business. *(A beat.)* You're turning that business around.

JEANNIE: It's not me, it's Warren. He's good at fixing cars, people really want to use him.

ASA: But you're the one keeping everything organized, doing the bills, ordering inventory. That little promo idea you came up with last month, "Spend two hundred dollars in repairs, get a free oil change"—how many new customers did you get with that deal?

JEANNIE: A few.

ASA: More than a few.

JEANNIE: I just like that we're doing it together.

ASA: I wish me and Rita had done more of that. Done something together, a business or a hobby. Things might have turned out different. *(A beat.)* When I was filling the truck up with gas today, Jimmy's mother was there. She was pretty drunk. She was trying to pump the gas but she kept missing her tank, gas was spilling all over the place. I felt sorry for her, so I went over to give her a hand. And I had the hose in the tank, I was pumping the gas, when she socked me in the arm.

JEANNIE: Oh my God.

ASA: She said, "It's all your fault, you son of a bitch. Your wife ran off with my kid, and it's all your fault."

JEANNIE: How is it your fault?

ASA: I'd rather not say.

JEANNIE: Okay.

ASA: How's that coffee?

(Jeannie jumps up and fills his mug. As he drinks, she stirs something on the stove.)

ASA: She said if I'd been more of a man, so to speak, Rita wouldn't have run off with Jimmy.

(A few beats. Jeannie doesn't know what to say. Asa stands up.)

ASA: How much time until supper?

JEANNIE: About thirty minutes.

ASA: I think I'll take a little drive over to Parker Road, see how they finished up their day.

JEANNIE: Okay.

(*He walks out into the front hallway, still carrying his coffee. Jeannie continues preparing supper as the lights come down. Lights come up, supper is ready. Warren comes into the kitchen from the front hallway.*)

JEANNIE: Wash your hands.

(*Warren goes to the sink.*)

WARREN: I'm washing them. (*A beat.*) So I stopped at the bank this morning, spoke to Jeff Crandall in the Loan Department.

JEANNIE: Warren—

WARREN: Just hear me out, Jeannie. (*A beat.*) Jeff said that based on how good the business is going, he thinks I might be able to get a small business loan.

JEANNIE: I thought we decided to wait on all of this.

WARREN: But so much is happening. I'm getting more customers every day, and it looks like I might actually land that service contract with the police. I'm outgrowing the shed, Jeannie. Denny wants to sell his business, and if I don't buy him out, someone else will. What if it's one of these chain operations and they start undercutting my prices?

JEANNIE: But we have to think about the baby coming, it's only three months away. We still have so much to buy, and we have to finish turning the upstairs bedroom into a nursery. All of that's going to cost a lot of money.

WARREN: And then there's Dad.

JEANNIE: I'm not talking about that.

WARREN: I am. I'm supporting my father for Christ's sake. This is not a good thing.

JEANNIE: Well he's not so happy about it either.

WARREN: Then why doesn't he get a job?

JEANNIE: He's tried.

WARREN: For about two minutes. Spends most of his time driving around town in his truck, stalking that California guy.

JEANNIE: Stop it.

WARREN: Where is he now?

JEANNIE: He said he'd be back in time for supper.

(*He sits down at the table, she brings him a beer. He grabs her, pulls her down to his lap.*)

WARREN: Come to the bank with me tomorrow. Let Jeff Crandall show you the figures. I think you'll be surprised when you see them.

JEANNIE: All right.

(They begin kissing. Asa comes in from the front hallway, Jeannie jumps off Warren's lap.)

ASA: Don't mind me.

(Jeannie begins serving supper. Asa sits down at the table.)

ASA: How's that coffee?

(She pours it for him.)

ASA: I've been hired.

WARREN: You got a job?

ASA: I did.

WARREN: Doing what?

ASA: Road crew. The California guy hired me.

WARREN: What?

ASA: He lost a fellow last week, so I applied for the job. I just heard, just a few minutes ago—I stopped by his office and he welcomed me aboard.

WARREN: You're going to work for him?

ASA: I am. I didn't want to say anything before, in case it didn't work out.

WARREN: The guy screwed you. He screwed you coming and going and now you're going to work for him?

ASA: Roads are all I know. And if it means working for the California guy so that I can get back to them, so be it. *(A beat.)* I haven't been too proud of myself these last few months. Being so dependent on my own son, that's not right.

JEANNIE But if it wasn't for you, Warren wouldn't have his own garage, so it all evens out.

(A few beats as everyone helps themselves to supper. Asa is suddenly overcome, he puts his fork down and starts to cry. Lights come down.)

SCENE II

Two weeks later. Lights come up full on the kitchen/den. Asa is alone, sitting at the table, drinking coffee. Jeannie comes in carrying a baby seat.

ASA: There you are.

JEANNIE: I'm sorry I'm late. *(A beat.)* I'll start the coffee.

ASA: I've already done it.

JEANNIE: You did?

ASA: *(Pointing at his mug.)* Not bad, if I do say so myself. *(He points at the baby seat.)*

ASA: That's a baby seat?

JEANNIE: I just bought it. Do you think it's silly to buy it now when the baby's not even due for another three months?

ASA: You're excited. Nothing wrong with that.

JEANNIE: Ready for lunch?

ASA: I am.

JEANNIE: Are sandwiches okay?

ASA: Sounds good to me.

(She starts making sandwiches.)

ASA: Warren won't be home for lunch?

JEANNIE: He's over at the police station, ironing out the details on the new service contract. *(She puts the sandwiches down, sits down with him.)*

ASA: Is he still mad at me?

JEANNIE: He's not mad at you. He's just never seen you cry before. He was surprised by it.

ASA: So was I. *(A beat.)* Can't believe how much he's accomplished this last year. First he gets the job working for Denny, then he opens his own garage—and now, now he's buying Denny out.

JEANNIE: I hope he isn't biting off more than he can chew.

ASA: Not with you behind him. You stick with him, he'll be fine.

(They begin eating.)

JEANNIE: So how is it working for the California guy?

ASA: I don't really see that much of him. In the morning we all meet and he gives us our orders for the day. Then we pretty much don't see him again until the next morning. Very different from the way I used to do things. *(A beat.)* Did I tell you I'm learning how to use a computer?

JEANNIE: No.

ASA: I am. There are three computers in the office now and we use them for all sorts of things. The California guy gives me a hard time for not knowing anything about them, says it's no surprise I'm not in charge anymore. I was holding the agency back, keeping it in the dark ages.

JEANNIE: He has some nerve.

ASA: *(Laughing.)* Oh he didn't mean anything by it. And he appreciates me, says no one knows the nature of roads like I do.

(A few beats. They are eating.)

ASA: Jeannie, do you know Dave Rogers who works on the road crew with me?

JEANNIE: Not more than to say "hi" to—he was a year ahead of me in school.

ASA: Do you think he's reliable?

JEANNIE: I guess so, why?

ASA: He came over to me this morning and said he saw Jimmy in a bar last week.

JEANNIE: Jimmy?

ASA: That's what he said. Apparently it was some bar over to the west side of Manchester.

JEANNIE: Is that where they're living?

ASA: That's what Dave Rogers tells me. Jimmy told him they rented a little apartment there. Rita is waitressing in a coffee shop and Jimmy's pumping gas somewhere. I asked Dave how he seemed, and he said he'd had a few beers but didn't particularly seem one way or the other.

JEANNIE: Did Jimmy mention Rita?

ASA: Just to say she's working in this coffee shop.

(Warren bursts into the kitchen from the front hallway.)

WARREN: Jimmy's mother—Jimmy's mother just shot Jimmy's father and the California guy's wife. She found them in bed together and she shot them.

(Lights come down.)

SCENE III

A week later. Lights come up full on the kitchen/den. Asa and Rita come in from the front hallway Asa is carrying a suitcase.

ASA: Warren and Jeannie were at the doctors this afternoon, they should be back around five.

RITA: I can just imagine what Warren will say when he sees me.

ASA: Oh, he'll be fine. *(A beat.)* Did I tell you he's buying out Denny Lawrence?

RITA: No.

ASA: Denny says he wants to retire early but I think it's really because Warren's taking all his customers. *(A beat.)* Remember when he asked us if he could open his garage in the shed? Good thing we didn't say no. *(A beat.)* I'll take this upstairs. *(He starts up with the suitcase.)*

(Rita moves slowly around the kitchen/den. She goes to the refrigerator, takes out a can of coffee, starts making it. She opens the refrigerator and inspects its contents. Asa comes back.)

RITA: I've started some coffee. *(A beat.)* And seeing if there's anything for dinner.

(*A beat.*) Hamburg. I could make meatloaf, only maybe it's too hot for meatloaf.

ASA: I don't think so. I think meatloaf sounds like a good idea. Maybe some of your mashed potatoes.

RITA: Are there potatoes? (*She looks in the cupboard.*) Just enough. (*She takes out the bag of potatoes.*) Did you go to Billy Reeves' funeral?

ASA: Yes.

RITA: Did Warren and Jeannie go?

ASA: Yes.

RITA: Jeannie's what, about six months along now?

ASA: I think that's about right.

RITA: It just seems like yesterday when Warren told us she was pregnant and wouldn't be going to college. I still can't believe she gave up her scholarship.

ASA: How's that coffee?

(*She glances over at the pot.*)

RITA: Not there yet. (*She is peeling potatoes.*) What about the California guy, did you go to his wife's funeral?

ASA: He didn't have it here, he had it in California.

RITA: Is it true he found them?

ASA: Yes.

RITA: I can't imagine. To find your wife shot ten times and with another man—I just can't imagine. I'd heard rumors about the two of them having an affair, but I thought it was a lot of gossip. (*A beat.*) Is he coming back to Tremont?

ASA: No. He's resigned from the agency, and his house is on the market. (*A beat.*) The town has asked me to step in.

RITA: Will you?

ASA: Don't really see how I can say no. (*A few beats.*) What about Jimmy, do you think he'll stay in Tremont?

RITA: I don't know. I haven't spoken to him since everything happened.

(*A few awkward beats.*)

ASA: Meatloaf and mashed potatoes, I'm looking forward to that. (*A beat.*) I've missed your cooking. (*A beat.*) Our Jeannie—she's a whiz at a lot of things, but cooking isn't one of them.

(*A few beats.*)

RITA: About a month ago there was an ad in the paper, an opening for a chef with a catering operation in Manchester. So I went and applied for the job. They asked me about my experience and if I had any training. I told them that I'd been cooking for my family since I was nineteen, but that wasn't what they were asking about. They said I wasn't qualified and the only thing they could offer me was some job bussing tables—

(Warren and Jeannie come in the front door.)

WARREN: What the hell—

ASA: Your mother's come home.

WARREN: She's not staying.

ASA: Don't be foolish. Of course she's staying. She's come home. She's making meatloaf and mashed potatoes for dinner.

(Jeannie turns to Rita.)

JEANNIE: Welcome home.

WARREN: *(To Jeannie.)* What the hell are you doing?

JEANNIE: I'm saying hello to your mother, why don't you say hello—

ASA: If we could just eat our supper and take some time to cool off—

WARREN: Jesus, I always knew you were a weak son of a bitch.

JEANNIE: Warren.

WARREN: But this—this is an all-time low. *(A beat.)* Wake up in the morning to find a goddamn note on your pillow, "I can't be married to you anymore. I've gone with Jimmy to start a new life. Don't try and find me." *(To Rita, laughing.)* Like we would even look. You weren't missed, Ma. We were doing just fine without you. Your leaving was the best thing that ever happened to this family.

JEANNIE: That's not true. *(To Rita.)* It's not, Rita.

WARREN: So what was it about Jimmy that turned you on, Ma?

RITA: I'm going upstairs.

(She walks toward the stairs, Warren blocks her.)

WARREN: Did you know he was a virgin? Did he tell you that? *(A beat.)* Jimmy Reeves, Jesus, Ma, you're pathetic. The two of you in bed together. Him crawling all over you—

(Asa takes his arm.)

ASA: That's enough.

(Warren shoves his father away.)

WARREN: Was his being a virgin a real turn on, Ma? Was it?

JEANNIE: *(Taking his arm.)* Let's go for a ride.

WARREN: I want her out of here.

JEANNIE: This is between your mother and father. Now come on, Warren.

WARREN: *(To Asa.)* Tell her to leave. Tell her to leave and never show her face again. Tell her, Dad. I want you to tell her. *Tell* her.

(A few beats.)

ASA: *(To Rita.)* I bought some fresh blueberries yesterday. Maybe you could bake a pie. I've missed your pie.
(Lights come down.)

SCENE IV

A few days later, late morning. Lights come up full on the kitchen/den. Jimmy comes in from the front hallway. He calls out to Rita, softly at first.

JIMMY: Rita— *(Louder.)* Rita— *(No response. He sits down at the table.)*
   (Rita comes in from the stairs. She is carrying a bottle of Windex and a roll of paper towels. She is quite startled to see Jimmy.)
RITA: What are you doing?
JIMMY: I was calling you.
RITA: I didn't hear you, I was cleaning the bathroom. *(She goes to pour herself some coffee.)*
JIMMY: I love you, Rita.
RITA: Asa's coming home for lunch. I don't want him to see you.
JIMMY: I went by our apartment this morning. But you weren't there. When did you leave?
RITA: Yesterday. I called Asa and he came and got me.
JIMMY: Just like that. You don't say anything to me first.
RITA: I came home from the coffee shop and you weren't there. You didn't even leave me a note.
JIMMY: I got the call about my Dad. I don't know what I was thinking, I just knew I had to get to the twins.
RITA: And you couldn't call me that night or the next day or the day after that.
JIMMY: There was so much to do. I was arranging the funeral, taking care of the twins. *(A beat.)* And my ma, I had to see her. I didn't want to, but she called me. She called me from the prison, crying and screaming. Saying how I had to come. *(A beat.)* So I go there. She starts all over again, crying and screaming. How he drove her to it, how Dad came to her and said the California guy's wife was different from all the other women he'd been with. He loved her and wanted to marry her, and Ma said she couldn't let him do that, that's why she shot him. *(A beat.)* I wanted to say to Ma, I was so close to saying, that maybe if she hadn't gotten so fat, maybe if she'd learned to cook a decent meal, none of this

would have ever happened. But I didn't. I didn't want her to start crying and screaming again. *(A beat.)* She asked me when I was coming back. I told her maybe some day next week. But I was lying, I'm not ever going back there. And she's never gonna see the twins again.

RITA: But she's their mother.

JIMMY: And she shot our father ten times.

(He goes to her, reaches out to her. They kiss. She pulls away.)

JIMMY: Are you really back here for good?

RITA: Yes.

JIMMY: Why?

RITA: Where else would I go?

JIMMY: With me. You'll come live with me and the twins at the house. I want us to be married.

(Rita can't believe what she's hearing.)

JIMMY: I've been thinking about it for days. We can get married, we'll live in the house. I'll take over Dad's business and you'll do your catering.

RITA: I already tried that, remember what happened?

JIMMY: I'm talking about starting your own business. *(A beat.)* I've got some extra money, from my Dad's life insurance, so I can even help you get started.

RITA: No.

JIMMY: Why not? I can't live without you, Rita. I love you so much. I need you. I need you now more than ever. *(A beat.)* Every day we're apart I get more twisted up inside. I'm sorry that I left like that, I'm sorry I didn't call. I will never do it again, I swear.

RITA: Jimmy, it's not just that. Things haven't been right for awhile now. You know that.

JIMMY: No I don't.

RITA: You were spending more and more time at that bar.

JIMMY: I won't do that any more, I will never go to a bar again.

RITA: Of course you will. You're nineteen.

JIMMY: No. If I can have you with me, I don't need stuff like that. I don't need bars, I swear to you. I'll make you happy.

RITA: Jimmy, we never should have run off together.

JIMMY: How can you say that? I love you and you love me.

RITA: Stop using that word.

JIMMY: Why, it's how we feel about each other.

RITA: No it's not Jimmy.

JIMMY: Don't tell me, I know how I feel about you. I love you. I love you. I love you. I love you.

RITA: Asa will be here any minute. I want you to go now.

JIMMY: No way. I'm staying here. And I'm telling him that you're coming with me. The two of you are getting a divorce and we're getting married.

RITA: We're not.

JIMMY: I'm not moving.

RITA: Jimmy, please—

(A few beats. Jimmy grabs her, kisses her. She pulls away, won't look at him.)

JIMMY: Rita—

(She still won't look at him. He storms out. She puts away the Windex, goes to the refrigerator to get food for lunch. The lights fade. Lights come up again. Asa comes in through the front door.)

RITA: I fell a little behind. I'll have your lunch for you in a few minutes.

(He sits down at the table. She brings him his coffee.)

ASA: Jimmy Reeves just passed me on the driveway.

RITA: That's because he was here. He asked me to come back to him and I said no. *(A few beats as she is making their lunch.)* I'm sorry, Asa—I'm sorry about everything, about everything that's happened, about everything that I've done. I'm very, very sorry.

(A few more beats.)

ASA: Maybe it would be a good thing if we didn't talk about this anymore. About you and Jimmy, about the last four months. *(A beat.)* We need to put all this behind us now, let things get back to the way they used to be. *(A few beats.)* How's that coffee?

(She pours his coffee as the lights fade to black.)

SCENE V

Three months later. Lights come up full on the kitchen/den. Rita is reading a newspaper. Jeannie comes in from the front hallway carrying her new baby, Charlie.

JEANNIE: Hiya.

RITA: Hi.

JEANNIE: I just have a few minutes. We're on the way back from the doctor's.

RITA: Is everything all right?

JEANNIE: Oh sure, just a checkup for Charlie. The doctor says he's healthy as a horse. *(A beat.)* I can't stay too long. Warren's expecting us home soon.

RITA: Stay until Asa gets here. He'll want to see you and the baby.

JEANNIE: Charlie, Rita. His name is Charlie.

RITA: I know.

JEANNIE: Then why don't you say his name? You're always calling him the baby.

RITA: I didn't realize. *(Rita goes over to the stove.)*

JEANNIE: What are you making?

RITA: Some gravy for the roast chicken.

JEANNIE: Oh, that sounds so good.

(Rita moves away from the stove, picks up the paper to show an article to Jeannie.)

RITA: I was reading this article on Frisbee throwers.

JEANNIE: Frisbee throwers?

RITA: Did you know that there are actual competitions for this sort of thing?

JEANNIE: No.

RITA: *(A beat.)* These people in the tournaments are really good. They can perform hundreds of tricks with the Frisbee. And there's a lot of prize money to win, they're even trying to get it into the Olympics. *(A beat.)* There are so many things in this world a person can be good at. It's just a matter of finding something and really working at it.

JEANNIE: Like you and cooking.

RITA: That's not the same thing. I just do a few simple things well. But as far as anything fancy, anything requiring real skill, I have no ability. *(A beat.)* When I was with Jimmy, I went to apply for a job at this catering operation. They practically laughed at me when I told them about my experience, they were looking for a professional, someone who can carve swans out of cheese dip. Cooking meals for my family didn't count. The only job available for me was bussing tables.

JEANNIE: Would you like to hold Charlie?

RITA: Not right now. *(A beat.)* What would you say you were good at?

JEANNIE: I'm a good mother.

RITA: You know that already? The baby, Charlie's—only a month old.

JEANNIE: When he was born, the minute they handed him to me, I knew I was meant to be a mother.

RITA: As soon as they handed him to you—

JEANNIE: Yes.

RITA: And you think that will be enough?

JEANNIE: I think it will be more than enough.

RITA: It's not too late, you can still go to college.

JEANNIE: Rita—

RITA: You could go part-time, take some night courses.

JEANNIE: I don't want to.

RITA: But you were such a good student.

JEANNIE: I said I don't want to. And please stop trying to make me feel bad about it.

RITA: I'm not.

JEANNIE: Oh yes you are. It's like you won't be happy until I say to you, "Rita, I've made a big mistake. I never should have married Warren. I never should have had Charlie. You were right all along." I think you want me to be miserable.

RITA: That's not true.

JEANNIE: Then be happy for me, Rita. Be happy for me. *(A beat.)* Why don't you go to college?

RITA: Oh be quiet.

JEANNIE: I'm serious. You're always telling everyone else to go. You go.

RITA: I'm thirty-nine.

JEANNIE: Oh that's so old.

RITA: I could never afford it. All we have is Asa's salary now. *(A beat.)* I even tried to get a few of my cleaning jobs back. But everyone has the same excuse, they've already hired someone else.

JEANNIE: You were gone awhile.

RITA: That's not it. No one wants me around, I go to the store to pick up some groceries or to the post office or the dump, and everyone gets so quiet. I can feel their eyes on me.

JEANNIE: It'll die down. Something else will happen, and people will start talking about that.

RITA: You keep saying that. But I don't know if people will forget, I think they have the idea that I'm to blame for everything, not just me and Jimmy running off but Jimmy's mother killing his father and the California guy's wife—

JEANNIE: Now that's paranoid.

RITA: I'm the only one left. Everyone else is either dead, in prison, or moved away. People need someone to blame.

JEANNIE: And what about Jimmy? If people are going to blame you, then why not him too?

RITA: People feel sorry for him. He has to be a father and a mother to the twins now. And people probably think I made him run away with me, that he had no say in it. *(A few beats.)* Is it true Jimmy's getting married?

JEANNIE: I heard something about it.

RITA: Who is she?

JEANNIE: Some girl he just met, I don't know anything about her.

RITA: Well I'm glad he's found someone.

JEANNIE: Are you?

RITA: Yes I am.

JEANNIE: Sometimes I can't help but wonder.

RITA: About what?

JEANNIE: If you still don't miss him. *(A beat.)* You never talk about him, not once since you've been back here have you talked about him, about the time you were with him.

RITA: And that means I miss him?

JEANNIE: Do you?

(A few beats.)

RITA: Right after I came back here, Jimmy came to see me.

JEANNIE: He came here, to this house?

RITA: Yes. He wanted me to move in with him and the twins. He wanted me to marry him.

JEANNIE: But you said no.

RITA: Of course.

JEANNIE: Why did you do it, Rita? Why did you take off with him? *(A few beats.)* You and Asa have been married for twenty years. You have a son. And no one, no one saw this coming. If you were so unhappy, why didn't you tell someone?

RITA: No one would have heard me.

JEANNIE: How do you know that?

RITA: I'd get up in the morning, I'd put on the coffee. I'd make breakfast. Then I'd go clean a couple of houses. I'd come home, make Asa his lunch, clean our house. Then I'd start supper, Asa and Warren would come home and eat supper, we'd watch some television. And if we were really lucky, you or Jimmy would stop by. If not, we'd go to bed and get up in the morning and start all over again. *(A beat.)* All that sameness, I couldn't stand it any more.

JEANNIE: So you take off with Jimmy Reeves?

RITA: I'd give Jimmy something to eat, he would tell me that I was the best cook in the world. I would tell him about an idea and he would actually listen. *(A beat.)* He said I was a star, a bright shining star.

JEANNIE: Oh, Rita.

RITA: You think I'm foolish.

JEANNIE: I just don't think you know how good you have it. Asa is a good husband, he only wants to see you happy. That's all he's ever wanted.

RITA: I'm here, aren't I? I'm cleaning his house and baking his pies.

JEANNIE: If you really want something more than that, then do something about it. *(Picking up the paper.)* If you don't think school is possible, look in the employment section, see if anything catches your eye.

RITA: I don't have any experience.

JEANNIE: Well maybe you should go back to that catering place and tell them you'll take the job bussing tables.

RITA: Why would I want to do that?

JEANNIE: It's a place to start, Rita.

RITA: I couldn't.

JEANNIE: Why?

RITA: *(Very sharp.)* I just couldn't.

JEANNIE: Suit yourself. *(A few beats.)* But I have to tell you, I'm getting really tired of all your complaining. It's getting so I don't even want to come over here any more.

RITA: Then don't. You're not supposed to be here anyway, Warren would have a fit if he knew.

JEANNIE: Is that really what you want?

    (A few beats.)

RITA: No—no, it isn't. *(A beat.)* Are you really happy?

JEANNIE: Yes. The only thing bad in my life right now is that Warren still won't see you and that Asa and Charlie and I have to sneak around.

    (Asa comes in through the front door. He lights up when he sees Charlie.)

ASA: There he is.

    (Jeannie hands Charlie to him.)

ASA: Grandpa's boy. *(A beat.)* Town gave me a raise today.

JEANNIE: Well, it's about time.

ASA: It's not a lot, but it won't hurt.

RITA: Congratulations.

ASA: Thank you.

    (Jeannie gives him a kiss on the cheek, takes Charlie back.)

ASA: How's Warren?

JEANNIE: Working hard.

ASA: I overheard a fellow say the other day that when it comes to having his truck fixed, if he can't figure it out, there's no one but Warren he can trust with it. He says Warren knows his engines and you don't ever have to worry about him cheating you.

JEANNIE: He really is good at what he does. Having the new shop and the extra space makes all the difference in the world. *(A beat.)* The other day when I was working on inventory, I answered the phone and this lady said she needed Warren to work on her car right away. I told her it would be at least two days before he could get to it. You know she started to cry?

ASA: Oh come on—

JEANNIE: I'm serious, she was crying. *(A beat.)* I told him he's going to have to think about hiring another mechanic.

ASA: Then he'll be someone's boss. What do you know about that?

RITA: Are you staying for supper.

(Jeannie gets up, taking the baby from Asa.)

JEANNIE: I can't. We're going out for pizza tonight.

ASA: Pizza.

JEANNIE: I wish you were both coming with us. *(A beat.)* I just hate this. I hate that we're all apart. I keep trying to talk to Warren, but he won't listen. Even my dad has talked to him, said it's time to let go of his grudge—if he doesn't, something might happen, and it would be too late.

RITA: What on earth could happen?

JEANNIE: You never know. And before you know it, it'll be twenty years and you still won't have spoken.

ASA: I'm going to call him tomorrow, take the first step.

JEANNIE: Oh Asa, that would be so good.

ASA: Doesn't mean he'll take my call.

JEANNIE: I think he might. It's one thing for him to call first, but if you call—
(A beat.) Rita—
(She says nothing.)

JEANNIE: Maybe you might call too.
(Rita still says nothing.)

JEANNIE: I'll let you get to your supper.
(She kisses Asa on the cheek again.)

JEANNIE: Thank you. *(She goes out through the front door.)*
(Rita is finishing setting the table.)

ASA: How's that coffee?
(She pours him some.)

ASA: So will you call him?

RITA: I guess you two have been thinking about this for awhile now.

ASA: I don't know.

RITA: Oh I do, it's very clear what happened here tonight. Jeannie comes by with the baby, the two of you have your casual conversation. And then suddenly you're calling Warren.

ASA: I had no idea she'd be here.

RITA: I don't believe you. You knew she'd be here and that she'd start talking about Warren. And you knew you'd decide to "give him a call" knowing she'd ask me to call too.

ASA: I'm tired of things being this way, I want them to go back to normal.

RITA: And what is normal?

ASA: You know what it is. *(A beat.)* There's Charlie to think about too. Let's put this behind us before he's old enough to have memories. If we do it now, he doesn't have to know that there was ever anything wrong. *(A beat.)* I want you to call Warren, tell him you're sorry. Tell him you're mother and son, and it's not right for you to be fighting this way.

(Rita doesn't respond. He bangs his fist down on the table. She jumps.)

ASA: Goddamnit, Rita. What is it? What is it that I'm doing wrong?

(She says nothing.)

ASA: Rita.

RITA: Don't you ever feel as though you've maybe missed something?

ASA: What on earth are you talking about?

RITA: That there's something very important out there for you, something that was meant for you all along.

ASA: Is that why you ran off with Jimmy?

RITA: That was part of it, yes.

ASA: But you didn't find it, did you?

RITA: No.

ASA: What is it that you're looking for?

RITA: I have no idea. *(A beat.)* I just know that something's missing.

ASA: How long have you been feeling like this?

RITA: For as long as I can remember.

ASA: Did you feel that way when we got married?

RITA: Yes.

ASA: Did you feel that way when Warren was born?

RITA: Yes.

ASA: Then why didn't you do something about it?

RITA: Because I had no idea what to do. *(A beat.)* Right before I graduated from high school I was having supper with my mother and father, my father asks me about my plans for the future. *(A beat.)* And then my mother says, "Maybe you'll marry Asa." So I nodded, and that was that.

(A beat.) We got married. Then I got pregnant with Warren and every day this restless feeling in me would grow. I would sit in this kitchen and wait for something to happen. I would wait for an idea to come to me about what to do, but it never came. *(A beat.)* I was so sure when Jeannie said she was pregnant and giving up college to marry Warren—I was so sure she'd end up feeling the way that I do. But she doesn't. She seems content. And I think she'll always be content. I don't understand that, why is she so content and I'm not? Why do you think that is, Asa?

ASA: I don't know.

RITA: When people see me now, when they speak of me, I know most of them talk about what a sad, foolish woman I am. And while that makes me want to hide in the house and avoid people, avoid their eyes, I don't know how I'll feel if they stop talking about me, if everything goes back to the way it was before. *(A beat.)* Someday, years from now, when I'm in the graveyard and someone happens to see my name on a gravestone they'll ask, "Rita Potter, who was Rita Potter?" Then they'll move on and my name will slip from their minds. And really it will be like I was never here at all. *(A beat.)* I suppose most people don't worry about that. Do you ever worry about it?

ASA: No. No I don't.

(Rita gets up from the table and goes to the stove. A few long beats.)

ASA: Do you think that one person can help another person find content-ment?

RITA: I don't know.

ASA: Would you let me try. *(A beat.)* Would you, Rita? Would you let me help you find contentment?

(A few beats.)

RITA: I'll serve supper now. I made a roast chicken.

ASA: All right.

(A few long beats.)

RITA: And there's gravy too. Would you like some gravy?

ASA: Sounds good.

(Rita begins serving him chicken and gravy. Lights fade.)

END OF PLAY

LYNNE ALVAREZ is a poet and playwright who has worked with the New Plays Program for several years. Her other new productions at A.C.T. include *The Reincarnation of Jaime Brown* (which was included in *Women Playwrights: The Best Plays of 1996*) and *Eddie Mundo Edmundo*. She has written and adapted over eighteen plays, which include *The Guitarron, The Wonderful Tower of Humbert Lavoignet, Hidden Parts, Thin Air: Tales from a Revolution,* a translation of Tirso de Molina's *Don Juan of Seville,* and of *The Red Madonna* by Fernando Arrabal. Her most recent play, *In the Dark,* is a murder mystery about class war. Ms. Alvarez has received various awards including the Le Compte de Noey Award, FDG/CBS, a Drama League Award, and a Rockefeller Fellowship. Ms. Alvarez is an alumnus of New Dramatists and is currently a consultant to the National Foundation for the Advancement in the Arts. Ms. Alvarez has published two books of poetry. Additionally, *Lynne Alvarez: Collected Plays* has recently been published by Smith and Kraus Publishers.

DAISY FOOTE is a nationally celebrated playwright, recently honored with the Roger L. Steven Incentive Award in association with the Kennedy Center Fund for New American Plays with support from the American Express Company in cooperation with the President's Committee for the Arts. Ms. Foote's plays include *Living with Mary, Farley and Betsy, Darcy and Clara, God's Pictures* (which had its world premiere at the Indiana Repertory Theater), and *The Hand of God,* which was developed with a commission from Wind Dancer Productions. Ms. Foote's screenplays include *My Name is O'Hanlen,* an adaptation of Willa Cather's *O Pioneers!,* an adaptation of *The Last Crop* by Elizabeth Jolley, and *The Love of Their Life* (to be directed by her husband, Tim Guinee). Ms. Foote's television work includes *The Edge of Nowhere,* a seven-part series for Turnabout productions in association with PBS and the Corporation for Public Broadcasting.

JIM GRIMSLEY is a playwright and novelist who lives and works in Atlanta, Georgia. He has written ten full-length and four one-act plays, including *Mr. Universe, The Lizard of Tarsus, White People,* and *The Existentialists.* He has been playwright-in-residence as Seven Stages Theatre since 1986. In 1988, he was awarded the George Oppenheimer/New York Newsday Award for Best New American Playwright for *Mr. Universe,* which was produced off-Broadway at the New Federal Theatre. Mr. Grimsley's novels *Winter Birds, Dream Boy,* and *My Drowning* have been published by Algonquin Books. *Winter Birds* won the Sue Kaufmann Prize for Best first Novel from American

Academy of Arts and Letters in 1995, and was one of three finalists for that year's PEN/Hemingway Award for best First Novel. *Winter Birds* and *Comfort and Joy* have also been published in Germany and France. Mr. Grimsley is a member of the Southeast Playwrights Project and Alternate ROOTS. Mr. Grimsley was recently awarded the first-ever Bryan Prize for Drama, presented by the Fellowship of Southern Writers for distinguished achievement in the field of playwriting.

BRAD SLAIGHT is a Los Angeles–based writer, actor, and comedian. As a writer, Mr. Slaight's stage plays have been produced all over the world and include *Class Action, Sightings, High Tide, The Open Road, The Eddy Show,* and *Halfway to Nowhere.* Additionally, Mr. Slaight has been on staff and written jokes and sketch material for many television shows including *The Tonight Show* (NBC), *Sunday Comics* (FOX), *Comic Strip Live* (FOX), *Into the Night* (ABC), *Just the Ten of Us* (ABC), and *Fact or Fiction* (MTV). Mr. Slaight's screenplays include *Close to the Kill* and *Front Runners.* Mr. Slaight wrote special comedy material for a National Lampoon CD-Rom and helped create an interactive program for Time Warner. Mr. Slaight's many television and film acting credits include starring roles in *Scream, Freshman Dorm, Married...With Children, Unsolved Mysteries, Out of Control, Second Cousin–Once Removed, Hellbent, Beakman's World,* and a two-year recurring role as Izzy Adams on *The Young and the Restless.* Mr. Slaight was an original member of the Comedy Store Players and is a founding member of the critically acclaimed comedy teams Moving Violations and Shecky Brothers.

CRAIG SLAIGHT is the Director of the Young Conservatory and New Plays Program at the American Conservatory Theater. As both a director and an acting teacher, Slaight has worked passionately to provide a creative and dynamic place for young people to learn and grow in theater arts. With a particular commitment to expanding the body of dramatic literature available to young people, Slaight has published eight anthologies with Smith and Kraus Publishers, *Great Scenes from the Stage for Young Actors, Great Scenes for Young Actors Volume II, Great Monologues for Young Actors, Great Monologues for Young Actors Volume II, Great Scenes and Monologues for Children, Multicultural Monologues for Young Actors, Multicultural Scenes for Young Actors,* and *Short Plays for Young Actors,* co-edited by A.C.T.'s Jack Sharrar. *Great Monologues for Young Actors, Multicultural Monologues for Young Actors,* and *Multicultural Scenes for Young Actors* were selected by the New York Public Library as Outstanding Books for the Teenage. Additionally, Slaight created the New Plays Program at A.C.T.'s Young Conservatory in 1989 with the mission to develop plays by professional playwrights that view the world through the eyes of the young. The first nine New Plays are collected in Smith and Kraus Publisher's *New Plays from A.C.T.'s Young Conservatory, Volumes I and II*. *Volume II* also received recognition from the New York Public Library as Outstanding Book for the Teenage in 1997. Educated in Michigan in Theater and English, Slaight taught at the junior and senior high school, college, and university levels, prior to moving to Los Angeles, where he spent ten years as a professional director (directing such notables as Julie Harris, Linda Purl, Betty Garrett, Harold Gould, Patrick Duffey, and Robert Foxworth). Slaight is currently a member of the Artistic Team at A.C.T. and frequently serves on the directing staff with the professional company. In addition to the work at A.C.T., Slaight is a consultant to the Educational Theater Association, the National Foundation for advancement in the Arts, and is a frequent guest artist, speaker, and workshop leader throughout the country. In August of 1994, Slaight received the President's Award from the Educational Theater Association for outstanding contributions to youth theater. In January of 1998, Carey Perloff chose Slaight to receive the first annual A.C.T. Artistic Director's Award. Slaight makes his home in San Francisco, California.